Nassau William Senior

American slavery

Nassau William Senior

American slavery

ISBN/EAN: 9783743377226

Manufactured in Europe, USA, Canada, Australia, Japa

Cover: Foto ©Suzi / pixelio.de

Manufactured and distributed by brebook publishing software (www.brebook.com)

Nassau William Senior

American slavery

A REPRINT OF

AN ARTICLE ON " UNCLE TOM'S CABIN,"

Mrs. Harriet Esther (Be

OF WHICH A PORTION WAS INSERTED

IN THE 206TH NUMBER OF THE " EDINBURGH REVIEW ;

AND OF

MR. SUMNER'S SPEECH

OF THE 19TH AND 20TH OF MAY, 1856.

WITH

A NOTICE OF THE EVENTS WHICH FOLLOWED
THAT SPEECH.

BY

NASSAÜ W. SENIOR, Esq.

LONDON :

T. FELLOWES, LUDGATE STREET.

1862

LONDON:
PRINTED BY R. CLAY, SON, AND TAYLOR, BREAD STREET HILL.

PREFACE.

THE following article was partially published in the "Edinburgh Review," during my absence from Europe. Considerable portions of the matter contained in the proofs, as I finally settled them, were omitted. It is now reprinted unmutilated, indeed verbatim, from the revise as it left my hands.

On re-perusal I have found nothing to soften or to retrench, though I could add and strengthen much.

I have also reprinted the speech of Mr. Sumner in the Senate of the United States, on the 19th and 20th of May, 1856, and a brief notice of the frightful scenes which followed it.

The moral and intellectual character of Mr. Sumner has long been admired by Europe.

To sympathy for his courage is now added sympathy for his calamity.

The result of the frightful scenes now passing in the United States must be much influenced by the conduct of the coloured race.

The following pages may afford some materials for conjecturing what that conduct will be.

SLAVERY

IN

THE UNITED STATES.*

THE sale of " Uncle Tom's Cabin " is the most marvellous literary phenomenon that the world has witnessed.

It came out as a sort of feuilleton in the " National Era," a Washington paper. The death of Uncle Tom was the first portion published, indeed the first that was written. It appeared in the summer of 1851, and excited so much attention, that Mrs. Stowe added a beginning and middle to her end, by composing and printing from week to week the story as we now have it, until it was concluded in March, 1852. It

---

* 1. *Uncle Tom's Cabin, or Life among the Lowly.* By HARRIET BEECHER STOWE. London: 1853.

2. *A Key to Uncle Tom's Cabin.* By HARRIET BEECHER STOWE. London: 1853.

3. *Sunny Memories of Foreign Lands.* By Mrs. HARRIET BEECHER STOWE. London: 1854.

4. *Speech of the Honourable Charles Sumner on his Motion to Repeal the Fugitive Slave Bill in the Senate of the United States.* Aug. 26. 1852. Washington: 1852.

B

was soon after reprinted at Boston in two volumes, — a form in which we have not seen it in England, although by the end of Nov. 1852, 150,000 copies had been sold in America. The first London edition was published in May, 1852, and was not large, for the European popularity of a picture of negro life was doubted. But in the following September, the London publishers furnished to one house 10,000 copies per day for about four weeks, and had to employ 1000 persons in preparing copies to supply the general demand.

We cannot follow it beyond 1852, but at that time more than a million of copies had been sold in England ; probably ten times as many as have been sold of any other work, except the Bible and Prayer-book.

All that we know respecting the sale in France is, that "Uncle Tom" still covers the shop windows of the Boulevards, and that one publisher alone, Eustace Barba, has sent out five editions in different forms. Before the end of 1852 it had been translated into Italian, Spanish, Danish, Swedish, Dutch, Flemish, German, Polish, and Magyar. There are two Dutch translations, and twelve German ones — and the Italian translation enjoys the honour of the Pope's prohibition. It has been dramatised in twenty forms, and acted in every capital in Europe, and in the free States of America.

Its moral influence, though it has not been as wonderful as its literary popularity, has been remarkable. In the form of a novel it is really a political pamphlet. It is an attack on the Fugitive Slave Law of America, and though it has not effected the repeal of that law, it has rendered its complete execution impossible.

Those among our readers to whom the subject is

not familiar may perhaps be interested by a short account of the origin, and the nature of that law.

Slavery is a status so repugnant to the principles of Christianity, that, though never formally abolished, it gradually died out, as, with the diffusion of knowledge and the improvement of intelligence, the spirit of our religion was better understood, and its precepts were better obeyed. By the beginning of the fifteenth century, it was practically extinct in the civilised portions of Europe. Its revival is one of the crimes of religious intolerance. At that time orthodoxy was supposed to be essential to salvation. The Church of Rome condemned to eternal damnation, as indeed she does now, all whose faith on any point, however practically unimportant, however purely speculative, however unintelligible, differed from the creed which she thought fit to proclaim. The Reformers followed her example. Each sect believed those, whose opinions varied from its own, worthy of the severest punishment which can be inflicted in this world, and destined to perpetual suffering in the other. The strongest term of reproach and antipathy in the English language, the word in which abhorrence and contempt are concentrated, is *miscreant.* That is to say, a person whose religious belief differs from that of the speaker.

When such was the sentence which each sect passed on its fellow Christians, — on men who agreed with them as to the precepts of Revelation, and differed from them only as to the essence of the Being from whom it was derived, or as to the nature of His relations to mankind, — of course they were not more merciful to infidels. The Roman Catholic, who condemned a Protestant to be burnt alive here, and to be tormented for never ending millions of years hereafter, had indeed nothing worse in store for the follower of Mahomet or of Menu. The difference seems to have been that they hated most the heretics and despised most the heathens. The former they treated as rebels, the latter as enemies. They believed the deities of Paganism to be real existences, to be devils in a state of permanent war with our Creator and Saviour, and their worshippers, therefore, to be the allies and auxiliaries of the enemies of God and of his people. They felt for them no more sympathy than we do for wolves or for tigers; in fact, they felt less, for, though we delight in killing a tiger, we have no pleasure in torturing one.

When it occurred, therefore, to the Spaniards, that the tropical regions of the new hemisphere, which were then mortal to the white labourer, might perhaps be profitably cultivated by seizing negroes in Africa, and transporting them to America, the cruelty or the injustice of thus treating the negro was not an element in the deliberation. He was a heathen, a worshipper of devils, a vessel of wrath, created for the purpose of enduring eternal misery, and to give him a foretaste in this world of what was to be his fate in the next, was only carrying out the decrees of Providence. The experiment was tried and succeeded. The English and the Dutch followed in this respect, as in her other colonial follies and enormities, the example of Spain. They were at that time the wisest and the most religious nations of the world. One of them had just conquered her independence and her freedom, the other was preparing for the long contest which ended in the British Constitution; but they had no more scruples about enslaving heathens than they had about enslaving horses.

These opinions, however, though they enabled the British settler to kidnap or purchase, and work to death, without compunction, the natives of Africa, did not justify retaining in servitude their children born in Barbadoes or Virginia, whom it was obviously his duty to educate as Christians, and, therefore, as equals in the sight of God to himself.

Another prejudice came to the aid of the planter's cupidity, and enabled him, as he thought, to reconcile his interests and his religion. The Bible was at that time considered by all, as it is now by many, as a single book, every word of which had been dictated by God. Little distinction was made between what Moses was forced by the hardness of his countrymen's hearts to tolerate, and what was a moral rule of general and eternal obligation. The laws which we now perceive to have been temporarily laid down for the guidance of semi-barbarians living under a theocracy, were then supposed to be also addressed to the fellow-countrymen and contemporaries of Bacon and Milton. Some of the New England States extracted from Exodus, Leviticus, and Deuteronomy, their municipal code, and fancied that they thus obtained institutions wiser than any that man could invent.*

---

* This error has been admirably illustrated by Archbishop Whately. "Christians acknowledge that the Mosaic Dispensation came from God; and that that, and also the Christian Dispensation, are contained in the volume which we call the Bible. Now any one who regards the Bible (as many Christians do) as *one book*, containing divine instructions, without having formed any clear notions of what does and does not belong to each dispensation, will of course fall into the greatest confusion of thought. He will be like a man who should have received from his father, at various time, a great number of letters, containing directions as to his conduct from the time when he was a little child just able to read till he was a grown man, and who should lay by these letters with care and reverence, but in a confused heap, and should take up any one of them at random and read it without reference to its *date* whenever he needed his father's instructions how to act." — *Third Dissertation prefixed to Encyclopædia Britannica*, pp. 509, 510.

Among these institutions was domestic slavery; palliated indeed in some respects when the slave was a Hebrew, but in others carried to its worst abuses.

" If thou buy an Hebrew servant," says the Book of Exodus, " six years shall he serve, and the seventh " he shall go free for nothing. If his master have " given him a wife, and she have borne him sons or " daughters, the wife and her children shall be her " master's, and he shall go out by himself. And if a " man sell his daughter to be a maid servant, she " shall not go out as the men servants do. If a man " smite his servant or his maid with a rod, and he " die under his hand, he shall be surely punished. " Notwithstanding, if he continue a day or two, he " shall not be punished: for he is his money." *

" Of the heathen that are round about you," says the Book of Leviticus, " shall ye buy bond men and " bond maids. Moreover, of the children of the " strangers that do sojourn among you, of them " shall ye buy, and of their families which they begat " in your land, and they shall be your possession. " And ye shall take them as an inheritance for your " children after you, to inherit them for a possession ; " they shall be your bond men for ever." †

It is impossible to deny that the law of Moses tolerated domestic slavery, that it tolerated the separation of families, and that it punished beating a slave to death only if he or she died under the infliction, or within a day or two after it.

Defoe was a man of eminent piety. He carries his hero, Colonel Jack, to Virginia, and leads him through all the gradations of colonial life from the state of a servant to that of an owner of slaves and plantations. He dwells on the wickedness of ill-

---

* Exodus, xxi. 2, 3. 7.   † Leviticus, xxv. 44—46.

treating slaves, but does not seem to have suspected that there could be anything wrong in buying, or keeping, or selling them.

One hundred and fifty years of peace and good government humanised and enlightened the stern bigoted Puritans and Catholics of our Western empire. The children of its aristocracy came to England for education ; they came to a country which boasted that its air could be breathed only by freemen. When they travelled on the Continent, they found slavery confined to its semi-barbarous districts, to its Sclavonic and Asiatic populations, — to Russia, Poland, and Turkey. They were told everywhere, and they must have felt it to be true, that the relation of master and slave was mischievous to both parties, hardening the heart, worrying the temper, and weakening the self-control of the one, and degrading the other into a brute, with all the vices of a man, and few virtues except the abject submission and unreasoning affectionateness of a dog.

The opinion grew that such an institution, though it might be Judaic, could scarcely be Christian, and by the time that the American colonies had achieved their independence, nearly all their great men had become earnest abolitionists. When, in the 14th of May, 1787, the Federal Convention met in Philadelphia to form a Constitution, the State of Massachusetts had already abolished slavery, and New Hampshire, Pennsylvania, Connecticut, and Rhode Island had provided for its gradual extinction by giving freedom to all future-born persons. Washington, though a slave-holder, declared that his suffrage in favour of the abolition of slavery should not be wanted. Franklin was president of an Abolition Society. Jefferson proposed, that by the Constitution slavery should be excluded from any territory to be

subsequently acquired by the Union ; a proposal
which, if it had been carried, as it was within a
single vote, would probably by this time have extinguished it : and Madison succeeded in excluding
from the Constitution the word ' slave,' lest it should
be supposed that the idea of property in man was
sanctioned by the American nation.

Two interests, however, united in favour of slavery.
The agriculturists of the South threatened to secede
from the Union if they were deprived of the population which afforded them the only means of culti-
vating their rice and indigo.   The maritime towns of
New England believed that their prosperity depended
on their retaining the American slave trade and the
American carrying trade.   A coalition between the
South and a part of the North was formed, with
slavery, slave trade, and a navigation law on its
banner, which the delegates from the remaining States
thought it dangerous to resist.

But it was supposed that the evil, though it must
be submitted to for a time, might be rendered temporary.   It was believed at that time, that slavery
depended on the slave trade.   The laws which regulate the increase of mankind were then little understood : the fear of depopulation was general, and it
was plausibly maintained that a race transplanted
from another hemisphere and a different soil and
climate, engaged in unhealthy occupations, and subjected to the depressing influence of slavery, would
gradually die out, if it received no reinforcements.
A clause was introduced into the Constitution, for-
bidding Congress to abolish the slave trade within
twenty years, and thereby impliedly giving it power
to do so at the end of that period.   This satisfied the
Northern capitalists, to whom twenty years seemed
an eternity.   It pleased the South, as it enabled them

to extend their cultivation and increase their gangs of negroes for nearly a quarter of a century, at the end of which time, if the slave trade were abolished, their estates and their slaves would enjoy a monopoly, since no fresh negroes could be introduced, and therefore, as they believed, no additional lands reclaimed.

The abolitionists felt that they were prolonging a national disgrace and a national crime; but they were convinced (as every one else was convinced) that at the end of the twenty years the slave trade must cease, and that slavery would not long survive it.

We have said that Madison succeeded in excluding from the Constitution the *word* " slavery ;" but it was thought necessary, with respect to three matters, to notice the *thing*. Two of these subjects were connected. They were, direct taxation and representation in the House of Representatives. It was agreed that these should both depend on population —that is to say, that each State should be taxed and represented according to its population.

The South maintained that, for the purpose of taxation slaves should be unnoticed— being not persons but chattels ; but that for the purpose of representation they should be counted, being, though chattels, chattels human. As a compromise, it was decided that, for both purposes, three slaves should be equivalent to two freemen. A compromise which now gives to the owners of three millions of slaves a representation equal to that to which two millions of freemen would have been entitled.

The third matter respected fugitive slaves. " Every " person," says the Constitution, " held to service or " labour in one State by the laws thereof" (the euphemism for a slave), " escaping to another, shall be

" delivered up on claim of the party to whom such
" service is due."

It does not appear that either this enactment, or
an Act of Congress passed in the year 1793, which
attempted to define the procedure by which it was to
be enforced, produced much effect. The surrender
was to be made through the instrumentality of the
State in which the fugitive was found. Such a duty
is a disgusting one. It is difficult to obtain its performance even as respects criminals. Though several
years ago England engaged, by a solemn treaty, to
deliver up to the French authorities Frenchmen accused of serious crimes, the French have not been
able up to this time to obtain from us, in a single
instance, the performance of the engagement. Every
one admits that the stipulations of the treaty are
wise, indeed necessary; but the case for the time
being before the Court is never within them. Some
States declined to pay any expenses incurred by their
officers in the execution of the law. In others, the
magistrates neglected to put it in force. A judge of
the Supreme Court of Vermont refused to admit any
evidence of ownership, " unless the master could show
a bill of sale from the Almighty."

In the mean time the slave trade was abolished.
Indigo and rice, the great staples of the slave States,
were produced more cheaply in India; and it seemed
probable that the Southern States would follow the
example of their northern brethren, and emancipate
their slaves, and thus fulfil the prophecy that the
extinction of slavery would follow that of the slave
trade.

Whitney, an obscure mechanic of Massachusetts,
falsified these expectations, by inventing, in 1793,
the saw-gin.

The long-fibred, or, in commercial language, long-staple cotton, of which the Sea Island is the best known variety, is cultivated with difficulty, and only on comparatively few soils. Much more than nine-tenths of the whole annual crop consists of the short-staple varieties. In these varieties the seed adheres so closely to the wool that, if they were to be separated by the hand, a man could not clean more than a pound a day. And even with the assistance of the rollers and the bow, which are now used for this purpose in India, and, until Whitney's invention, were employed in America, the expense is so. great that scarcely any — we believe, indeed, none — of this cotton was exported from America while that process was necessary. The whole export in 1793 was only 187,000 lbs., probably consisting exclusively of long-staple cotton. The saw-gin was introduced, and in 1794, the very next year, the export was about decupled — it rose to 1,601,760 lbs. The next year it advanced to 6,276,300 lbs.; in 1800, it was 17,789,803 lbs.; in 1810, it was 93,261,462 lbs.; and in 1852, the last year for which we have the returns before us, the export of the short-staple variety alone exceeded one thousand one hundred millions of pounds.

The cotton plant flourishes best in alluvial lands in the neighbourhood of the sea, and cannot endure a mean summer temperature lower than 77° Fahrenheit, or a mean annual temperature lower than 60°. On the Atlantic coast of America, the 35th parallel, and towards the western coast, the 39th, are the most northern latitudes in which it can be cultivated. But no climate is too hot for it. The south-west of Texas, where the mean summer heat is 85°, suits it well. It belongs, therefore, to climates and to soils unfavourable to the constitutions of men of northern descent, if out-door work be required from them. In such climates field labour is disagreeable to all men, and dangerous to whites.

If the Anglo-Americans had been in the situation of an European community, surrounded by powerful nations, and subject to the restraints of international law and of international morality, South Carolina and Georgia, the only cotton-producing districts of the original Confederation, would soon have been fully peopled. Virginia, Maryland, Kentucky, North Carolina, and Delaware,—in all of which the white man can work,—would have followed the example of the Northern States, and have gradually emancipated their slaves. Slavery would have been confined to the two Southern States, and would have existed in the mitigated form in which it was seen in our West Indian islands ; the cause, of course, of occasional cruelty and of constant oppression and degradation, but free from the worst of all the abominations of modern American slavery, the breeding and exporting system,—the system under which the principal use made of men and women is to produce and bring up children, to be torn from them as soon as they attain the age of sale, and never to be seen or heard of again.

But the neighbours of the United States were dependencies of distant empires or semi-barbarous or barbarous republics. France sold to them all her subjects and all her territories in Louisiana. Spain sold to them Florida. The vast territories which now form Arkansas, Mississippi, Alabama, and Florida, were in the possession of their aborigines, Creeks, Cherokees, Choctaws, Chickasaws, and Seminoles, to whom they had for the most part been guaranteed by treaty. But what is the value of a treaty between the weak and the strong, in a country in which the very name of international morality is unknown ?

The Indians were removed to the north, and a district three times as large as the British Islands was added to the Southern States. Texas was a portion of the defenceless incoherent Mexican republic. American speculators swarmed into it, and got up a rebellion against the central authority. The American Government acknowledged the rebels as an independent nation, and immediately accepted from them a cession of the country. Mexico remonstrated, and was punished for her insolent want of submission by war, defeat, and mutilation.

The United States were thus more than doubled in extent, and, what was more important as respects slavery, the greater part of the newly-acquired territory was so nearly tropical as to be better suited to the coloured races than to the white. Their first acquisition, Louisiana, was already a slave country; so was Florida; but the Mexican Government had abolished slavery in all its dominions, and a negro slave never had existed in the Indian country, except in a few instances among the Cherokees. As soon, therefore, as the Union was to be increased by the introduction of new States, the question arose whether slaves should be excluded from a soil which, so far as it was peopled, was peopled by freemen. It was first tried in the case of Missouri. The contest began in 1818, and lasted for three years. Twice the House of Representatives voted the exclusion of slaves from the new State. Twice the Senate, which assumes to be the Conservative portion of the American Legislature, and, like its brethren in Europe, is the patron of every old prejudice and abuse, voted their admission. At length the anti-slavery party were deluded into accepting what was called the Missouri compromise, by which Missouri was received as a slave State, but the existing Congress affected to bind their successors by enacting that in future slavery should not be established to the north of latitude 36° 30'.

To understand this contest, we must remember that, in 1808, the African slave trade had ceased. Up to the time it had been vigorously prosecuted. Between 1790 and 1810 the number of slaves increased from 697,897 to 1,191,364, notwithstanding the emancipation of about 120,000 negroes in the Northern States, and notwithstanding the preponderance of males which is incidental to every migration, voluntary or compulsory. An almost unlimited supply of slaves ceased nearly at the time that the acquisition of a new nearly tropical empire produced an almost unlimited demand.

Few of our readers can be ignorant of the means by which that demand was met. It was met by a new slave trade, more cruel, more degrading, more atrocious, than that which had been abolished. The total number of slaves in Virginia in 1840 was 448,886. During the ten years ending 1850 the slave population of the United States increased at the rate of 28 per cent. The number of slaves in Virginia, therefore, in 1850, ought to have been 574,574; it was only 473,026. Instead of increasing at the rate of 28 per cent., the slaves in Virginia increased at the rate of only 5½ per cent. Instead of adding 125,688 to their numbers, they added only 24,140. What became of the missing 101,548? It cannot be answered that they were not born, or that they died. The climate of Virginia is one of the best in the world; the labour in the plantations is light; the negroes are well taken care of. Every traveller admires the number of healthy children. If the natural increase of the slaves in the whole Union was 28 per cent., that in Virginia was probably 35 or 40 per cent.

The question, what became of the missing 101,548, is answered when we look at the rate of increase in the States which are consumers instead of breeders, when we find that in Louisiana the increase was 44 per cent., in Mississippi 57 per cent, and in Arkansas 135 per cent. It is to these States, and to Texas, Alabama, and Florida, that Virginia has exported her human crop; it is from them that she has received, at the low average price of 500 dollars per head, fifty millions of dollars for her 100,000 souls. It was to preserve this trade, that Mexico was robbed of Texas, and afterwards of California and New Mexico; that Cuba is to be snatched and Jamaica to be annexed; and that every new State in which the climate is suited to the negro, is admitted unto the Union as a slave State.

Few things have more surprised the world than the deterioration of the political men of America. When the United States were a mere aggregate of scantily peopled colonies,—when their principal citizens were planters, shopkeepers, and traders, trained up in the narrowness and prejudices, and petty employments of provincial life, they produced statesmen, and negotiators, and administrators, and legislators, whose names will be for ever illustrious in history. Now that they form a great empire, that they possess a large class of men born in opulence, to whom all the schools and universities of each hemisphere are open, who have leisure to pursue the studies and to acquire the habits of political life, few of their public men would pass in Europe for tolerable second-rates. This downward progress, however, seems now likely to be arrested. We do not expect to see the present tenant of the White House succeeded by a first magistrate inferior to himself in knowledge, in ability, or in statesmanship, or the American diplomatists now resident in the Courts of the Continent, followed by men of less tact, or temper, or good sense.

We believe that the explanation of this strange depravation is to be found in the influence on American parties of the political questions connected with slavery.

A party which aims at producing only one result by only one means, has an enormous advantage over its rivals, who seek to promote the general welfare of their country. Sincerely patriotic parties are necessarily divided. Though they cannot but agree as to the end that is ultimately to be attained, it is equally certain that they will differ as to the means that are to be employed. Their common purpose is one that can be effected only imperfectly. It is composed of many elements, some of them opposed to others; the conduct which promotes the public prosperity in one respect, may impede it in another. A public man has to choose often between irreconcilable advantages, often between incompatible evils. It is difficult to predict the consequences of a new measure, and still more difficult to find believers in the prediction. It is very seldom, therefore, that two parties, each of which desires above all things the general good government of the country, can coalesce. Each is wedded by original disposition, by association, by habit, and by the desire of consistency to opinions and measures inconsistent with those to which the other is equally chained.

The selfish single-purposed party, to which general politics are indifferent, which is ready to ally itself to Freetraders or to Protectionists, to Reformers or to Anti-Reformers, to Puseyites or to Dissenters, becomes powerful by becoming unscrupulous. If Ireland had been an independent country, separated from England, the Ultra-Catholic party, whose only object is the domination of the Clergy and of the Pope, would have ruled her.   This is the source of the influence of a similar party in France.   The Clerical, or Jesuit, or Popish, or Ultra-montane faction,— whatever name we give to it,— has almost always obtained its selfish objects, because those objects are all that it cares for.   It supported the Restoration, its priests blessed the insurgents of February 1848, and it now worships Louis Napoleon.   The only condition which it makes is Ecclesiastical and Popish supremacy, and that condition the Governor for the time being of France usually accepts.

Such a party is the Southern party in the United States.   Its only object is the retention and extension of slavery and of the internal slave trade.   For this purpose, it is ready to ally itself to Whigs or to Tories, to Democrats, or to Federalists, to those who wish to raise, or to those who wish to lower, the tariff.   But this is a purpose which must excite the fears of every wise man and the detestation of every honest man.   All the best men of America, therefore, resist the contamination of such an alliance.   They see that the Southern faction, by choosing its opportunities, by joining from time to time the party that will accept its terms and can triumph by means of its assistance, generally obtains its objects, rewards its favourites, and excludes its opponents.   Most of them are discouraged, and forsake political life for literature or business, or foreign travel; others are cut short in their public career, and forced to resign themselves to provincial or professional eminence.   A few, like the distinguished senator whose speech we prefix to this Article, acquire fame in the Senate or in the House of Representatives, but are excluded from office.   And what, on this side of the Atlantic, are the prizes of public life, the high political and ad-

C

ministrative posts, are generally left to the inferior
men, whose ignorance, violence, or incapacity have
led those who judge of America only through her
public servants, to look on her with unmerited contempt or disgust.

We say "unmerited," because we believe that the
public morality of the educated classes in America,
who take no part in politics, is generally far superior
to that of the great bulk of her statesmen.   For the
proof of this, we need not go further than to " Uncle
Tom" itself.   It is a purely American work.   When
it first appeared in the columns of a newspaper, the
author looked only to a narrow local circulation.
When it was reprinted, the American market only
was thought of.   Mrs. Stowe did not address herself,
like Washington Irving, or Prescott, or Wheaton, to
an European public.   She wrote only for Americans,
and writing for them she poured out her sympathy
with the weak and the humble, her indignation
against the oppressor, her obedience to justice, and
her adoration of liberty, in words as bold and as uncompromising as any that were ever uttered by Milton, or Fox, or Wilberforce. She does not discuss the
highest principles of human conduct, she assumes
them : she takes for granted that they are not only
known to her readers, but professed by them.   If
" Uncle Tom" were still only in manuscript, and it
had been shown to us, with the information that an
American lady intended to publish it in America, we
should have said, " The readers for whom that book
" is intended, must enjoy a high civilisation and great
" moral and intellectual cultivation.   They must be
" religious, just, and humane. If they form part of an
" empire tainted by slavery, they must be impatient of
" the disgrace, and alarmed by the sin."   And the
result would have more than justified us, as it has
more than justified Mrs. Stowe.

We must admit, however, that Mrs. Stowe, writing from personal observation, draws a dark picture of the influence of slavery, and of the slave trade, on a portion of her countrymen who take no part in active political life.

We copy a part of one of her letters, dated Paris, August, 1853:—

" There is one thing which cannot but make one
"indignant here in Paris, and which, I think, is keenly
"felt by some of the best among the French; and that
" is the indifference of many Americans, while here, to
" their own national principles of liberty. They seem
" to come to Paris merely to be hangers on and ap-
"plauders in the train of the man who has overthrown
"the hopes of France. To all that cruelty and injustice
"by which thousands of hearts are now bleeding, they
"appear entirely insensible. They speak with heartless
"levity of the revolutions of France, as of a pantomime
" got up for their diversion. Their time and thoughts
" seem to be divided between defences of American
" slavery and efforts to attach themselves to the skirts
"of French tyranny. They are the parasites of para-
" sites—delighted if they can but get to an imperial
" ball, and beside themselves if they can secure an in-
" troduction. Noble-minded men of all parties here,
"who have sacrificed all for principle, listen with sup-
" pressed indignation while young America, fresh from
" the theatres and gambling saloons, declares, between
"the whiffs of his cigar, that the French are not capable
"of free institutions, and that the government of Louis
" Napoleon is the best thing that France could have.
" *Thus, from the plague-spot at her heart, has America*
"*become the propagandist of despotism in Europe.* No-
" thing weighs so fearfully against the cause of the
" people of Europe as this kind of American influence.
" Through almost every city of Europe are men whose

" great glory it appears to be to proclaim that they
" worship the beast and bear his name in their fore-
" heads. I have seen sometimes, in the forests, a vigor-
"ous young sapling which had sprung up from the roots
"of an old, decaying tree. So, unless the course of
" things alters much in America, a purer civil liberty
" will spring up from her roots in Europe, while her
" national tree is blasted with despotism." *

Our own experience does not enable us to confirm
Mrs. Stowe. The Americans with whom we have
been sufficiently intimate to enable us to ascertain
their political opinions have been enlightened and
liberal men, who differed from us, so far as they differed from us at all, rather by their republican, than
by their despotic, tendencies. They were in general
partisans of the revolution of 1848, and looked forward with hope to the triumph of the Montagne in
1852. Most of them approved of the Hungarian
insurrection, and, in their vehement detestation of
Austria, seemed to wish to see her join Russia against
England and France, in the hope that we might
attack her by an Italian rebellion. Others were so
indignant at the prevalence of despotism throughout
the Continent as to expect with pleasure a general
revolutionary war. Mrs. Stowe's experience is much
wider than ours, which is, in fact, confined to nine
or ten individuals. She probably came across ten
times as many. We do not venture to question the
acuteness of her observation, or the accuracy of her
report.

We must add that the sympathy with Russia
which has been manifested by some of the inhabitants
of the Southern States, supports Mrs. Stowe's remark, that the defenders of slavery in America na-

* Sunny Memories, vol. ii. letter 48.

turally become the enemies of freedom in Europe.
The good sense and the liberality of the opinions of a
neutral may generally be tested by the side which his
wishes take in the present war.

The people, that is to say, the mass of the inhabitants of Europe, are anti-Russian. There are, indeed,
among the Poles, Italians, and Hungarians, men
whose hatred of Austria leads them to desire her
defeat and humiliation at any expense. They know
that if Russia succeeds, Austria loses her independence. Some of them probably hope that she will be
partitioned, and that Russia will create out of her
wreck a new semi-Russian kingdom of Poland, and a
new semi-Russian kingdom of Hungary, and will
allow Italy a quasi-independence under her Protec-
torate. And they are mad enough to prefer the
scorpions of Russia to the whips of Austria.

But these fanatics form a small minority. The
people of Europe are, we repeat, anti-Russian. They
see that wherever Russian power, or even Russian
influence extends, it brings with it repression, ignorance, religious intolerance, the slavery of the press,
commercial restriction, and every other oppression
by which improvement can be arrested and Europe
forced back into a barbarism worse than that of the
dark ages, as the barbarism of communities that have
once been civilised is more corrupt and more hopeless
than that of a race that still retains, like our Saxon
ancestors, the vigour and independence of their still
less civilised progenitors.

The Continental despots and their courtiers look
forward to Russian preponderance with expectations
similar to those of their subjects ; but, with the
intense selfishness which belongs to power ill acquired
or ill used, the greater part of them desire it on the
very grounds on which their subjects dread it. They

believe, as the Russian Government itself believes, that knowledge, toleration, self-respect, freedom of the press, freedom of trade, freedom of intercourse, — in short, all that raises man intellectually and morally, is favourable to the object of their hatred and terror, political liberty. Hence their love of Russia, as the type and the supporter of what they call order, — as their faithful ally in their struggle against improvement, — as the great and generous friend, whose ready sympathy can always be relied on by a king, or a prince, or a grand duke, at variance with his subjects, and whose active aid will be given as soon as the interference of England and France is no longer to be feared.

The slave holders and slave traders of America are too strong to need to look for assistance to Russia; but they sympathise with her partly for some of the reasons which govern the petty tyrants of Italy and Germany, and partly for reasons of their own. They hate England as abolitionist, as Ferdinand hates her as liberal. They love Russia, as he does, for her intolerance of liberty and knowledge. And there is between the two countries the strong bond of similarity of institutions. Russia and the Southern States of the American Union are the only civilised slave holders left in the world. Slavery in Russia is indeed far milder, and far less diffused, and it is gradually wearing out. But while it lasts Southern America has the countenance of one companion.

As an illustration of the prevalent feeling, we copy from a New Orleans paper of the 15th January, 1855, the following extract from a speech addressed by the Rev. Ch. R. Marshall, Chairman of the Committee of Education, to a convention of delegates from the Southern States.

The speaker reprobated the practice of educating

Southern children in the North. "Our sons and
"daughters," he said, "return to us with their minds
"poisoned by fanatical teachings and influences against
"the institution of slavery."

"The reverend speaker," continues the reporter,
"then considered slavery as an institution, and passed
"upon it a glowing eulogium as contributing to the
"glory in arts and sciences, in religion, and national
"prosperity, in all countries wherein it has ever ex-
"isted. He described it as forming a part of the
"patriarchal system of government, established by
"God himself, as having been countenanced by Christ,
"and argumentatively sustained and practically sup-
"ported by the chief of Christ's Apostles, St. Paul.
"He (the speaker) had proclaimed these opinions in
"the streets of New York, and of Boston. He be-
"lieved slavery to be right, and that within fifty years,
"instead of decreasing, it would be double in extent
"to what it now is. He believed that the colonies
"now gathering on the coast of Africa would all be
"Slave States."

"In the course of his speech," adds the reporter,
"Mr. Marshall, commenting on the hostility of Eng-
"land towards our institutions, drew forth loud de-
"monstrations of applause by expressing the hope,
"very earnestly, that the Czar would triumph in the
"pending war in the East."

We return from this digression to the great subject of "Uncle Tom," — the most striking, though
perhaps not the most important, of the recent triumphs of the Southern party, — the Fugitive Slave
Law of 1850.

We have seen that little effect was given to the
clause in the Constitution directing that "persons
held to service in one State and escaping to another
shall be delivered up to the party to whom such ser-,

vice was due." The disinclination of the local authorities in the free States to enforce the law against a fugitive, the evidence as to the claimant's title, as to the servitude of the person claimed, and as to his identity, which they vexatiously required — the protection and concealment, and often the active assistance, which he received from the religious and the humane, — and the expense of the legal proceedings, and of the escort which was sometimes necessary to prevent a rescue on the road, and to detain the fugitive at night, were the chief obstacles to the efficiency of the Act of 1793.

The Act of 1850 endeavours to remove them. It directs the circuit Courts of the United States to appoint Commissioners, "with a view to afford reasonable facilities to reclaim fugitives from labour."

It enacts that the owner of a fugitive or his agent may pursue and reclaim him, either by obtaining a warrant, or by himself seizing and arresting him, and may then take him before a commissioner, whose duty it shall be to determine the case *summarily*, and, on proof by deposition or affidavit of the title of the claimant, and the identity of the fugitive, to grant to the claimant a certificate, which shall authorise the claimant or his agent to remove such fugitive back to the State whence he or she escaped. "IN NO TRIAL OR HEARING, UNDER THIS ACT," it continues, "SHALL THE TESTIMONY OF SUCH ALLEGED FUGITIVE BE ADMITTED IN EVIDENCE."

On affidavit of the claimant, or of his agent, that he fears a rescue, an officer of the court is bound to undertake the removal of the fugitive to the State whence he escaped, and to require such assistance as he may think necessary, and is to be repaid all his expenses out of the treasury of the United States.

The marshals and deputy marshals of the United

States are bound to assist under a penalty of 1000 dollars, and are liable in the full value of the fugitive if he escapes from them. The persons executing the Act are directed to call in aid all bystanders and the *posse comitatus*, and all good citizens are commanded to assist them.

The commissioner is paid by fees, *and receives* 10 *dollars if he grants his certificate, but only* 5 *if he refuses it.*

Every person obstructing a claimant, or attempting to rescue a fugitive, or harbouring, or concealing, or assisting him or her, directly or indirectly, to escape, is, for each such offence, to pay to the United States a fine of 1000 dollars, and to be imprisoned for six months, and moreover is to pay by way of civil damages to the owner 1000 dollars for each slave thereby lost to him.

Lastly, any owner of a fugitive slave may apply to any Court of Record in his State, whereupon the judge, on being satisfied as to the ownership, and the slave's escape, is to make a record of the facts, and a description of the fugitive, and to deliver to the applicant a transcript of such record. " Which transcript," says the Act, " shall be held and taken to be full and conclusive evidence of the fact of the escape, and that the service or labour of the person escaping is due to the party therein mentioned." The production of this transcript, together with other evidence, *if necessary*, of the identity of the person claimed, to a commissioner in any other State, entitles the claimant to a certificate, authorising him to seize or arrest and transport the person claimed to the State from whence he escaped.

No time is a bar. A man who has been settled for thirty years in a northern city, who has a family and a profession, who has forgotten that he ever was in bondage, or perhaps who never *was* in bondage, may be dragged before a commissioner, bribed by a double fee to condemn him, and, on affidavit that *A. B.* is a slave, and that he is *A. B.*, may, without being heard in his defence, for the Act expressly declares that he shall not be heard, be *summarily* sent into slavery for life.

Even this mockery of a trial is not necessary. Under the last clause in the Act, *A. B.* living in Charleston, hearing that there is in Philadelphia one *C. D.*, whom he would like to appropriate, has only to go to the Charleston Court, and obtain a transcript of a record describing *C. D.*, and stating that he is *A. B.'s* fugitive slave. On showing this transcript in Philadelphia, and making oath as to *C. D.'s* identity, he is entitled to a Philadelphian certificate, with which he may proceed to *C. D.'s* house, and without warning, summons, or trial, seize him, bind him, gag him, and carry him as a slave to Charleston.

America calls herself free, but such oppression is not to be found in Naples or in Russia. What security has any coloured person, what security indeed has any white person, under such a law as this ?—under a law by which he can be declared a slave in his absence, on an *ex parte* application, and receive the first notice that his freedom has been questioned from those who handcuff him as a slave ?

It is said that the Southern States frightened the Northern States into acquiescence, by threatening, if their monstrous bill were rejected, to renounce the Union. We cannot understand how such a threat should have been effectual. Had we been Northerns, *we* should have used it, and we should have acted on it, instead of submitting to it. We should have said, " Rather than be the accomplices and the victims of " such a tyranny, we separate. We are already a great

" nation, in a few years we shall be a great empire,
" free from a stain which debases us at home and
" disgraces us abroad."

We say the *victims*, as well as the accomplices, for
under the provisions of this law on what tenure does
an American hold his freedom ?   What stands between him and slavery ?   Not a trial, not a regularly
constituted court, not the verdict of a jury, not an
appeal, not even a writ of habeas corpus.   He may
be torn from his home, from his friends, and from his
family, and subjected to a punishment far worse than
the scaffold of Robespierre or the knout of Nicholas,
by a procedure, and on evidence, which in England,
we should not think sufficient to decide the title to a
dog, or to warrant the stopping up of a footpath.

The penalties on aiding or concealing a fugitive, or
directly or indirectly obstructing a slave hunter, must
render anxious the life of every man of common
humanity who lives near the line of a fugitive's escape.   Those penalties are, to men of the moderate
fortunes common in America, absolutely ruinous.
Yet who when he rises in the morning can say, that
he shall not render himself liable to them in the course
of the day, or of the night ?   Few Englishmen,—we
hope few Americans,— who had to choose between
the incurring those penalties and the turning out a
fugitive helpless before his pursuers, would hesitate.
But what can be said of the freedom of a country
which has submitted to a law which exposes all its
citizens to the alternative of imprisonment and ruin,
or of eternal unavailing remorse ? *

We have said that " Uncle Tom " is, in fact, under
the disguise of a novel, a pamphlet against the Fugitive Slave Law.   Such is Mrs. Stowe's account of it.

" For many years of her life," she says, " the

* See Note I.
* c 6

" author avoided all reading upon, or allusion to, the
" subject of slavery, considering it too painful to be
" inquired into, and one which advancing light and
" civilisation would certainly live down.   But, since
" the Act of 1850, when she heard with consternation
" Christian and humane people actually recommending
" the remanding escaped fugitives into slavery as a
" duty binding on good citizens ; when she heard on
" all sides from kind, compassionate, and estimable
" people in the free States of the North, deliberations
" and discussions as to what Christian duty could be
" on this head,—she could only think, these men and
" Christians do not know what slavery is; if they did,
" such a question could never be open for discussion.
" And from this arose a desire to exhibit it in a living
" dramatic reality.   She has endeavoured to show it
" fairly in its best and in its worst phases. In its best
" aspect she has perhaps been successful: but oh, who
" shall say what yet remains untold in that valley and
" shadow of death that lies on the other side ?" *

Its political influence has been little less remarkable than its literary success.   Though the Fugitive
Slave Law excited the indignation of many persons
belonging to the higher classes in the free States, it
was not unpopular among the people.   The contempt, the loathing, with which the coloured race is
avoided in those States, deprives of all public sympathy every one that is suspected of being stained by
the least drop of black blood.   No one, who has not
been raised by a better education far above ordinary
prejudices, looks on a negro, or on the descendant of
a negro, as a fellow creature.   For the first two years
after the passing of the Act, the lower classes in New
York and Boston enjoyed the excitement of a negro

* Chapter 45.

hunt as much as our rustics enjoy following a fox
hunt. Nor is it likely that the mere reading of the
novel would have much affected them. But it was
dramatised and acted in the Bowery Theatre in New
York. The hero and heroine of the piece were Eliza
and George. The great scene was Eliza's passage up
the Ohio. It was well got up and well acted. When
she leapt the turbid torrent, and dashed over the
cracking ice, leaving her amazed pursuers on the
bank, the theatre rung and rung with applause. For
150 successive nights this scene was acted in New
York, and we have no doubt that it was repeated in
the other free States. The sovereign people was
converted; public sympathy turned in favour of the
slave. A few months ago a fugitive was claimed in
Boston and remanded to slavery. Such was the fear
of a rescue, that all the national army that could be
collected,—a tenth, we believe, of the whole military
force of the Union,—was called out. Files of in-
fantry with loaded muskets surrounded the court
house, and lined the streets that lead from it to the
wharf where the vessel that was to carry him off lay.
Cannon were placed to command the cross streets,
all business was suspended, the balconies were covered with black cloth, and the bells of the city tolled,
as the steamer with its captive left the shore.

The attempt will not be repeated. As far as the
Northern States are concerned, "Uncle Tom" has re-
pealed the Fugitive Slave Law.

Having related the strange story of "Uncle Tom's"
success, it is now our duty to endeavour to account
for it,—to ascertain and explain the causes, intrinsic
and external, which have given to it a popularity
which this generation cannot deny, because it has
witnessed it, but which our posterity will be tempted
to treat as fabulous.

The first of these causes we believe to be the subject.

It describes the state in which millions of persons speaking our language, professing our religion, and, in many cases, not distinguished from us by colour or by feature, within a fortnight's steam of our shores, are now, at this instant, placed, and may remain placed, for an indefinite time. It is a state of which we have no experience, and which probably now exists for the first time since the creation of the world.

Of course, the slavery which we describe as now existing for the first time, is that of the slave-breeding States, not that of the slave-consuming ones. The slavery of Alabama or of Texas exhibits only the ordinary and known features of slavery: heightened, perhaps, by differences of race and colour, and by the deep-seated antipathy of the American towards the Black; but probably not worse, perhaps better, than that which prevailed in the last century in our own West Indian islands.

It is the slavery of Maryland, Virginia, Kentucky, and North Carolina, which resembles nothing that was ever seen before.

The African slave trade was frightful, but its prey were savages accustomed to suffering and misery, and to endure them with patience almost amounting to apathy. The victims of the American slave trade have been bred in a highly cultivated community. Their dispositions have been softened, their intellects sharpened, and their sensibilities excited by society, by Christianity, and by all the ameliorating but enervating influences of civilisation. The savage submits to be enslaved himself, or have his wife or his child carried off by his enemies, as merely a calamity. His misery is not embittered by indignation. He suffers only what, if he could, he would inflict. He cannot imagine a state of society in which there shall not be

masters and slaves, kidnapping and man-selling, cof-
fles, and slave traders; or in which any class shall be
exempt from misfortunes which appear to him to be
incidental to humanity.

The civilised Virginian, who can never go from his
cabin with a certainty of spending another night in
it; who can never part from a child with a certainty
that he shall see it again; who, at any moment,
without any preparation, may be told, "Follow that
man — you are sold;"— who, without fault, and without warning, has to leave a home and a family, and to
pass the remainder of his life, among strangers, in a
distant land, a burning climate, a pestiferous air, and
perhaps under a brutal master;—the Virginian wife,
who sees her husband handcuffed and carried off, because his good conduct, industry, and skill have made
him so valuable that his master thinks that he cannot
afford to keep him;—the Virginian mother, who
finds that her children, one after another, disappear,
as each attains the age of sale, and the sooner in proportion to their intelligence and beauty;—all these
feel their sense of suffering sharpened by their sense
of wrong. All around them are whites, their fellow-
countrymen, their fellow-subjects, and their fellow
Christians, whose homes are inviolable, among whom
the child belongs to its parents, husbands and wives
to one another, and a man to himself. To the black
race alone, and to their descendants, all family ties
and all security are denied; domestic affections, the
greatest source of happiness to the rich, almost the
only source of happiness to the poor, are to them
converted into instruments of torture, into the causes
of constant anxious terror, and of occasional anguish
and desolation.

In Europe we were all aware of the existence of
the causes of these abominations; but, until we were

roused by " Uncle Tom," we had not, to use a convenient Americanism, " realised" their results. We
wanted no " Key to Uncle Tom's Cabin " to convince
us, that if the laws of a country place two races in
the relation of proprietor and property; if the race
which is property is more cheaply propagated and
raised in one part of that country, and more profitably worked in another; no obstacle, raised merely
by benevolence or by pity, can prevent the human
stream from seeking to find its level, from flowing
from the territories in which man is abundant and
cheap, to those in which he is scarce and dear. But
though we possessed the outline of the scene, we
wanted its colouring and details. These Mrs. Stowe
has given to us; her pictures carry with them the
excitement of novelty as well as the weight of truth.
The great authoress has put into our hands a tele-
scope, by which the coloured races are brought so
near to us, that we can see them in their labours and
in their sports, in their sufferings and in their enjoy-
ments, in their insecure happiness—if any state that
is insecure deserve to be called happiness—in their
terrors, and in their despair. We do not wonder at
the crowds that have been collected by a spectacle so
strange without being surprising, so unlike anything
that ever was seen before and yet so obviously real.

This accounts for the difference between the fortunes of " Uncle Tom," and of Colonel Senior's remarkable novel " Charles Vernon." *   " Charles Vernon " was as graphic and as accurate a representation
of slavery in Jamaica, as " Uncle Tom " is of slavery
in America. But Colonel Senior described slavery
not as it is now, but as it was forty years ago. Events
similar to those which he painted had long ceased to

* See the review of " Charles Vernon," Edin. Rev. for January,
1849. Vol. 89. p. 83.

occur, at least in the country in which his scenes were
laid.   His picture was valuable to the historian, and
interesting to the moral observer; but it wanted the
present reality of "Uncle Tom."   The reader of
"Charles Vernon" was instructed and amused, but
he was not excited.   The reader of "Uncle Tom" is
roused to action.   He feels that if he can contribute
anything—and there are few who can contribute
nothing—towards abating, or even mitigating, the
monstrous system that is exposed before him, he is
guilty if he remains quiescent.

Next in importance to the attractiveness of the
subject is the attractiveness of the moral colouring
with which Mrs. Stowe has lighted it up.   The reader
always sympathises with the writer, and always feels
himself the better for doing so.   It is difficult for a
poet not to paint himself while he thinks that he is
describing only the creatures of his imagination.   No
one can read "Amelia," or "Persuasion," without
seeing who sat for the principal character.   We rise
from "Don Quixote" as well acquainted with Cer-
vantes as with the knight of the rueful countenance.
This is peculiarly the case with Mrs. Stowe; as her
work is as much a piece of rhetoric as of poetry—in
fact, is more so.   She is more anxious to persuade
than she is to please.   The moral, which is absent
from most poems, and, where it exists, is generally so
concealed as to be discovered only on reflection, is
prominently exhibited in every chapter of "Uncle
Tom."   Now it has been admitted from the times of
Aristotle, that the great instrument of an orator is
the ἦθος τοῦ λεγοντος; that the speaker whom you believe to be sincere, and with whose feelings you sympathise, has already half persuaded you.   "Uncle
Tom" possesses both these means of influence, and

D

much in its highest excellence. It is obviously an honest book. Some of the answerers of Mrs. Stowe accuse her of having overcoloured her pictures. Admitting her to have done so, no candid reader can think that she has done so intentionally. There is nothing exaggerated or artificial in her loathing of cruelty, in her indignation at oppression, or in her scorn of the wretched sophistry with which they are palliated or even defended. Her descriptions and her declamation are as much the relief of a mind which seeks vent for the sense of misery and wrong, as they are among the means by which that misery and wrong may be mitigated. And the reader can no more refuse to her his sympathy than he can his confidence. She has all the loftier and all the humbler virtues. She is bold, high-minded, and enthusiastic. She is kind, tender, and affectionate. And over her character is spread a tint of piety which softens and refines and harmonises the whole. New Englander as she is, there is nothing austere or ascetic, or menacing in her religion. It is a religion of hope and of love, not of fear or of denunciation. Present assistance and future reward are constantly promised: temptation and punishment are kept out of sight. Our Saviour appears in every page : the existence of Satan is almost ignored, except, indeed, when she makes the negroes assign to him the duty of taking the slave traders who tear children from their parents. "For if the devil don't get them, what he good for?" No sectarian doctrine, no sectarian feeling intrudes. If we did not know that "Uncle Tom" has been prohibited by the Pope, we should have supposed that there was no form of Christian faith in which it would not find grateful admirers.

Its defect, in the eyes of his Holiness, was perhaps the omission of the especial object of his adoration, the Madonna. If Mrs. Stowe had been a Romanist, the Madonna would have taken the place of Jesus Christ : the majestic vision " as of one crowned with thorns, buffeted and bleeding," which to Protestants seems a bold, almost a rash invention, would have been turned into the Queen of Heaven, glorious and triumphant ; and would have passed among Roman Catholic readers as a real and probable incident.

It is possible, too, that the Papal authorities were alarmed by hearing of one of the effects produced by the work in Paris—a general demand, among the ouvriers, for bibles. The bouquinists have assured us, that during the year 1853 they were the books most in request. All the stalls were full of them ; and the purchasers, to most of whom the book was unknown, asked anxiously whether what they were buying was the " real bible,"—" Uncle Tom's bible ? "

When we give the first place, among the causes of Uncle Tom's popularity, to its subject, we speak of its European popularity. We believe that the principal cause of its American popularity, was its religious colour. In the New England States there is a general dislike, or rather a general dread, of works of fiction. Among Puritans, the fear of evil predominates over the hope of good. Any source of pleasure, which may also be a source of pain, is prohibited. They think it safer, perhaps easier, to be abstinent than to be temperate. Novels give much amusement, and good novels give some instruction ; but the reading, even of good novels, is easily carried to an excess which is always injurious to the mind, and often to the character. A total abstinence, therefore, from novel reading pervades New England. " The anti- " slavery of Uncle Tom," says a Boston critic, " rather " hurt it than otherwise ; and, in spite of all its re- " markable merits of execution, but for its appeal to

" the religious sensibilities of Christendom, its admir-
" able realisation of the popular ideal of the Christian
" hero, saint, and martyr, it would, perhaps, scarcely
" have been known out of the small circle of anti-
" slavery readers, or, at least, the not large circle of
" novel readers, instead of sweeping away, as it has
" done, thousands upon thousands who never read a
" novel before in their lives, and who had even been
" accustomed to hold prose fictions in abomination."

Even in this country in some classes, particularly
among the Dissenters, novel reading is forbidden, and
here, as in America, " Uncle Tom " is excepted from
the general prohibition. It is difficult for those who
have not been subjected to this ascetic interdiction of
works of imagination, to estimate adequately the effect
of such a story on minds to which the intoxicating
stimulus of fiction was unknown. It must have been
to them like light given to those blind from birth,—
the revelation of a new sense.

We cannot dismiss Mrs. Stowe's religion without
remarking that a question, which puzzled Job and
Solomon, seems much to perplex her,—How to reconcile moral and physical evil with the attributes
of the Deity.

" ' If you only trust in God,' says Eliza to George,
" ' He'll deliver you.'

" ' I can't trust in God,' he answers. " ' *Why does*
" ' *he let things be so?* '

" ' There is no use,' says Cassy to Tom, " ' in calling
" ' on the Lord.—He never hears : there isn't any God,
" ' I believe ; or if there is, he's taken sides against
" ' us.' "

" We pass," says Mrs. Stowe in her own person,
" Kinsale, where the ' Albion ' was lost. I well re-
" member when a child the newspapers being filled
" with the dreadful story of the wreck. How for hours,

" rudderless and helpless, they saw themselves driving
" with inevitable certainty against these pitiless rocks;
" and how, in the last struggle, one human being after
" another was dashed against them in helpless agony.

" What an infinite deal of misery results from man's
" helplessness and nature's inflexibility in this one mat-
" ter of crossing the ocean ! What agonies of prayer
" there were during all the long hours that this ship
" was driving straight on to these fatal rocks, all to no
" purpose ! It struck and crushed, just the same.
" Surely, without the revelation of God in Jesus, who
" could believe in the Divine goodness ? I do not
" wonder that the old Greeks so often spoke of their
" Gods as cruel, and believed that the universe was
" governed by a remorseless and inexorable fate." *

The only solution seems to be that physical evil,
and, what is much worse than physical evil, moral
evil, exist because they cannot be prevented; or, in
Bishop Coplestone's words, " That God is not the
author of evil, although he is the author of every
thing else." † *Why* they cannot be prevented,—*why*
it was that the sacrifice of our Saviour was necessary
in order to mitigate them,—we cannot discover, and
we are not told. Perhaps the impossibility of pre-
venting evil may depend on causes which our faculties
are incapable of comprehending. But that there *is*
such an impossibility, both reason and revelation,
when they teach us that the Deity is benevolent,
compel us to believe.

We have shown how much of the popularity of
" Uncle Tom" arises from its appealing to our
sympathies. We fear that we must add that much
of that popularity arises from its also appealing to our

---

* Sunny Memories, chap. 2.   † Coplestone's Discourses, p. 93.

antipathies. The anti-slavery feeling in America is less diffused than it is in Europe, but it is more intense. Scarcely any man can proclaim himself an abolitionist without having to make a considerable sacrifice of popularity, perhaps of fortune. Even those who stop short of abolition, but are unfavourable to the extension of slavery into territories as yet free from it, have to play a losing game—a contest which strongly tasks the temper and the charity of the player; which may bind him closely to his own cause, but is certain to embitter him against that of his opponents; which may make him love his friends, but cannot fail to make him hate his enemies. To men in this state of mind "Uncle Tom" was a god-send. Mrs. Stowe came like a heavenly auxiliary, like the divine Twins at the battle of the Lake Regillus, or St. Jago in the van of Cortez, using weapons such as they had never thought of, wielded with a skill which they did not possess. She showered on the supporters of the Fugitive Slave Law and of the extension of slavery, invective, ridicule, contempt, and defiance, with arrows winged by genius, and barbed and pointed, and poisoned by truth. The anti-slavery party would have been more than men if they had not welcomed with enthusiasm, such an ally, — if they had not deified the amazon who, if she had not led them to victory, at least had given them revenge.

The evil passions which "Uncle Tom" gratified in England were not hatred or vengeance, but national jealousy and national vanity. We have long been smarting under the conceit of America — we are tired of hearing her boast that she is the freest and the most enlightened country that the world has ever seen. Our clergy hate her voluntary system — our Tories hate her democrats — our Whigs hate her parvenus — our Radicals hate her litigiousness, her insolence, and her ambition. All parties hailed Mrs. Stowe as a revolter from the enemy. She came to us knowing all the weak points in his camp, all the gaps in his line. She taught us how to prove that democrats may be tyrants, that an aristocracy of caste is more oppressive than an aristocracy of station ; and, above all, that a clergy supported by their flocks is ready to pervert the fundamental principles of Christianity to suit the interests or the prejudices of their paymasters. The malevolent emotions, as is the case with all our instinctive feelings, have their pleasures, but in civilised life we seldom can fully enjoy them. This explains the delight that men feel in battle. There is something intoxicating in the vent suddenly given to passions that have always been smothered, in the power suddenly acquired to kill and to plunder, to gratify anger, revenge, and rapacity, with a good conscience. Something like this is felt when the sins of a rival nation are held up to us : we revel conscientiously in the excitement of contempt and anger. Our pity for the victim is swallowed up in our hatred of the tyrant. To the gratification of our indignation we add the gratification of our pride. We look at the atrocities of the internal slave trade, and of the Fugitive Slave Law, and rejoice that no such crimes stain the British Islands. We read the laws prohibiting instruction, prohibiting the acquisition of property, and prohibiting emancipation, and congratulate ourselves on the reception which such legislation would have encountered if it had been tendered by a British colony for the approbation of a British sovereign. We thank God that " we are not even as this publican."

Another source of the popularity of " Uncle Tom" is its naturalness. It has no plot, no *peripateia*. The

fortunes of the different *dramatis personæ* move on in
separate lines, little influencing one another, without
the elaborate entanglement and clever unravellings to
which we are accustomed in fiction. The events are
connected rather by time than by causation. In few
incidents does the hand of the inventor betray itself:
one of these is the sudden death of St. Clair after he had
begun, and before he had completed, the forms necessary to the enfranchisement of Tom. It is ushered in by
a note of preparation and warning, which an experienced novel reader cannot misunderstand. First, we
are told that he has begun to take the necessary legal
steps. Then his cousin Ophelia warns him of the
calamities which may befal his favourite slaves if he
should die before he has provided for their future
fate. Then St. Clair laughs at her *post mortem*
speculations, and revolves vast indistinct schemes of
making some effort to rescue his country from the
disgrace of slavery, and goes out to be back in an
hour. Then Tom thinks of his home, and how soon
he shall be a free man, and be able to return to it at
will. He feels the muscles of his brawny arms, and
rejoices that they will soon belong to himself, and
work out the freedom of his family, until his meditations are cut short by those who bring back his
master wounded and dying. This long preface is
too obviously artificial. Indeed, the event itself is
too obviously artificial. A novelist has always the
power of bringing on a catastrophe by an unexpected
opportune death, but it is the very facility of this
expedient that renders it objectionable. Such an
accident is so frequent in fiction and so rare in
reality, that its introduction dissipates the temporary
illusion which the poet endeavours to produce.

George's story is more than artificial, it is improbable. Mrs. Stowe gives to him the talents and

habits of a highly educated man, and the manners and carriage of a gentleman. How he acquired advantages which in England are supposed to be the result only of early and careful cultivation, and of constant contact with equally cultivated associates, he tells us himself: " I grew up," he says, " long, " long years,—no father, no mother, no sister; not a " living soul that cared for me more than a dog; no- " thing but whipping, scolding, starving. Why, sir, I " have been so hungry that I have been glad to take ·" the bones they threw to their dogs; and yet when I " was a little fellow and laid awake whole nights and " cried, it was'nt the hunger; it was'nt the whipping " I cried for.   No, sir; it was for my mother and my " sisters; it was because I had not a friend to love me " upon earth.   I never knew what peace and comfort " was. I never had a kind word spoken to me till I " came to work in your factory. Mr. Wilson, you " treated me well, you encouraged me to do well, and " to learn to read and write, and to try to make some- " thing of myself; and, God knows, how grateful I " am for it."

A few years spent in Mr. Wilson's factory turn him out at twenty-five an accomplished man—a man whose exterior is so striking as to impress a whole company instantly with the idea of something uncommon.   Either the manners of an American gentleman are much more easily acquired than those of an English one; or there must be in races enriched by negro blood a wonderful affinity for refinement.

He naturally rises to be the most useful servant in the factory to which his owner, Harris, has hired him out.   He invents machinery, for which his proprietor takes out a patent, and becomes invaluable to his immediate employers. His owner hears of his success, is indignant that a slave should be marching round the country, inventing machines and holding up his head, and takes him away, in spite of remonstrances and high offers, to waste his talents and accomplishments in the lowest field drudgery.

Harris's brutal folly seems to us as unnatural as George's refinement. He has had no quarrel with his slave. For several years the only relation between them has been that he has found George a property of great and increasing value. Yet, merely out of spite at the "smartness" of a negro, he resolves to destroy this property, and to reduce an instrument, which was worth to him perhaps 200*l.* a-year, and might become worth much more, to one scarcely paying for its keep.

Mrs. Stowe certainly produces a succession of striking pictures, by exhibiting a slave, of the highest intelligence and cultivation, exposed to the most degrading oppression; but she does it by accumulating impossibilities.

In general, however, the illusion of reality is admirably kept up. Scene after scene follows, without effort, without dulness, and without exaggeration, in which every character acts and talks as we expected him to do. One of the elements of the naturalness of the story is the absence of love; that is, of love between unmarried persons, for of conjugal love, of parental love, and of religious love, there is abundance. Mrs. Stowe is to be added to the very small list of great poets who have attempted to interest the reader without the aid of a pair of lovers. That the attempt is an arduous one may be inferred from its rarity, and that rarity gives to "Uncle Tom" a double advantage. The ordinary reader observes the absence of one of the badges of fiction : the critic admires the genius and the courage of the writer who has dared to compose a novel, making no use of the material which is supposed to be the staple of novel writing.

Perhaps this contributed almost as much as its piety to its reception in New England. The sorrows of husbands and wives, parents and children, were read without fear by those who would have been scared if they had been seduced into sympathy with a lover and his mistress. " Uncle Tom " could not be excluded as a love story.

We have said that the actors in " Uncle Tom " act and talk as we expect them to do. To recur, however, to a classification on which we ventured when reviewing Thackeray's novels,* — the characters are generally simple : that is to say, characters to whom only a few qualities are given, all of which combine to lead their possessor into one line of conduct.

Uncle Tom, for instance, is simply perfect. Not a particle of human infirmity is allowed to profane his excellence. He is pious, affectionate, brave, honest, intelligent, confiding, humble, — in short,. he is composed of every Christian virtue and grace without alloy.

Eva is also perfect. Her whole character is formed of youthful love and piety.

Marie is another simple character. She is made up merely of intense selfishness and weak intelligence. Haley, Harris, Eliza, Legree, — in short, each of the *dramatis personæ*, except Ophelia, St. Clair, and Topsy, is coloured with an uniform tint. Those who are wicked have no virtues, those who are good have no vices. This certainly impairs the naturalness which we have mentioned as one of Mrs. Stowe's

* See the Number for January, 1854.

merits. The absurdity of ascribing perfection to human beings is felt more forcibly as respects Tom and Eva, when we recollect the circumstances of which this perfection is the result. The only associates of Eva, besides her parents, are slaves ; a race who, as Mrs. Stowe complains in every page of her book, are, by virtue of their social position, ignorant, degraded, and depraved. From whose example or instruction did she get her glowing piety, her seraphic love, or her angelic purity ? from Mammy, or from Rosa, or from Adolph, or from her dreamy infidel father, or from her hateful mother ? If the *status* of slavery be so debasing, how did Uncle Tom become a hero and a saint ? How was it that the greatest possible excellence, or, to speak more correctly, excellence greater than is possible, was produced by the worst possible education ?

But though this mono-chromatic colouring — this absence of shade where there is light, and of light where there is shade — is an artistic defect, we are not sure that it may not have contributed to the popularity of the work. The mass of readers seek only to indulge their sympathy and to gratify their curiosity. They are often rather annoyed than pleased when faults are attributed to their favourites, or merits to those whom they have determined to hate. They like to divide the inhabitants of the land of fiction, as they generally do those of the land of reality, into good and bad, silly and clever; and are disappointed by the

      "Fears of the brave and follies of the wise."

They like to understand what they read. Prospero and Miranda are comprehended at a glance : Hamlet is an enigma not yet satisfactorily solved. And for one reader of "Hamlet" there are a hundred of "The Tempest."

We have said that Miss Ophelia rises above the somewhat monotonous uniformity of Mrs. Stowe's characters; but her peculiarities are rather of manner than of substance. She is a strong-minded, clear-headed, unimpassioned New Englander, with an accurate perception of her duties and a firm resolution to perform them. The qualities which individualise her are, an exterior preciseness and coldness, concealing warm affections; and a sympathy for the slaves, as oppressed and degraded, somewhat at variance with her national antipathy to them as negroes.

The great merit, however, of Ophelia is as a contrast to St. Clair. He is drawn with a much bolder outline, and finished with much finer details. The foundation of *her* character is conscientiousness; the foundation of *his* is benevolence. Her defect is a want of imagination; his is a want of self-control. She endeavours to be useful only to the circle of persons with whom she is in immediate contact; and she succeeds. Her object is a small one, but it is accurately marked out. She knows what she wishes to do, and what are the proper means, and she employs them resolutely, perseveringly, and efficiently. St. Clair's purposes are vast and lofty; they are to affect the fortunes of millions of human beings, through centuries after centuries; but they are vague and undefined. He looks on the existing state of his country with horror, and on his own share in maintaining it, with repentance. A half-formed resolution to reform it is never absent from his mind. But his meditations seldom carry him beyond a wish—never beyond a hope. He never advances even so far as to form a definite plan; but drifts on, amiable, intelligent, but useless; doing no harm to his slaves, except by over-indulgence, but doing them little good ; and, from mere indolent procrastination, leaves them, when he dies, to the chances of sale, and to the miseries of slavery, aggravated by the lax discipline and careless kindness to which he had accustomed them. His levity is characteristic, of a mind ill at ease. He is gay because he cannot trust himself to be serious. An attempt at indifference is his only resource against fierce indignation or remorse.

A horrible case of slave-murder occurs :

" ' It is perfectly outrageous,' " says Ophelia to him: " ' It will bring down vengeance upon you.'

" ' My dear cousin,' " he answers, " ' I didn't do it, and " ' I can't help it. I would if I could. If low-minded " ' people will act like themselves, what am I to do ? " ' They have absolute control — they are irresponsible " ' despots. There would be no use in interfering. " ' There is no law that amounts to anything, practi- " ' cally, for such a case. The best we can do is to " ' shut our eyes and ears, and let it alone. It is the " ' only resource left to us.'

" ' How can you shut your eyes and ears ? How " ' can you let such things alone ?'

" ' My dear child, what do you expect ? Here is a " ' whole class, debased, uneducated, indolent, provok- " ' ing, put, without any terms or conditions, entirely " ' into the hands of such people as the majority of " ' the world are; people who have neither considera- " ' tion nor self-control, who have not even an enlight- " ' ened regard for their own interest — for that's the " ' case with the largest half of mankind. Of course, " ' in a community so organised, what can a man of " ' honourable and humane feelings do but shut his " ' eyes all he can, and harden his heart ? I can't " ' buy every poor wretch I see. I can't turn knight- " ' errant, and redress every case of wrong in such a

" ' city as New Orleans.   The most I can do is to try
" ' and keep out of the way of it.' " *

The rest of the conversation, with the exception of
some socialist nonsense about capitalists starving their
work-people to death, is a fine piece of rhetorical
poetry.   It is admirable as a history of St. Clair's
mind, and still more admirable as a condensed, lumi-
nous picture of the system, made still more odious by
its apologists, which he has too much virtue to tolerate, and not enough to resist.

St. Clair's scepticism is well conceived.   His mind
is one of those on which religion is easily impressed.
He is sensitive, affectionate, and imaginative.   He is
educated by a mother whose virtues and talents he
inherits, and whose piety he imbibes while he is under
her influence.   But his religion, founded on feeling
not on reasoning, fades away when he goes out into
the world, and finds the Bible habitually quoted as
an authority for systematic cruelty and oppression.
His scepticism is not described as arising from his
having thought that he had discovered any defect in
the evidences of Christianity, for it does not appear
that he ever examined them.   It does not seem to
occur to him, — indeed it does not seem to occur to
Mrs. Stowe, — that faith ought to repose on conviction, and that conviction is an affair not of the heart
but of the intellect.

His attempts to combat his doubts by his wishes
are well painted.

" ' Oh,' " says Tom to him, " ' if mas'r would only
" ' look up, where our dear Miss Eva is, up to the
" ' dear Lord Jesus.'

" ' Ah, Tom, I do look up; but the trouble is, I
" ' don't see anything when I do.   I wish I could.   It

* Chapter 19.

" ' seems to be given to children and poor honest fel-
" ' lows like you, to see what we can't.'

" ' Thou hast hid from the wise and prudent and
" ' revealed unto babes,'" murmured Tom.

" ' Tom, I don't believe — I can't believe — I've got
" ' the habit of doubting,'" said St. Clair; "'I want
" ' to believe this Bible, and I can't.'

" ' Dear mas'r, pray to the good Lord,—do, do,
" ' dear mas'r, believe.'

" ' How do you know there's any Christ, Tom? you
" ' never saw the Lord.'

" ' Felt him in my soul, mas'r, — feel him now.'" *

Even Mrs. Stowe does not seem to perceive that
she has engaged her hero in a contest in which, as he
manages it, success is impossible. Minds unaccus-
tomed to reasoning, habituated to bow to authority,
and to take their opinions on trust, may believe because they are told to believe, or because they have
always believed, or because those about them believe,
or because it is happiness to believe, or because it
is a sin not to believe. But reasoners, men who cannot accept conclusions without premises, however they
may wish to be satisfied without proof, cannot be so.
And the more earnest their desire, the more certain
is their failure. The more they wish to arrive at a
given conviction, the more anxious becomes the crav-
ing for evidence, the more arduous seem the difficulties that are to be got over, the more obstinate are
the lurking doubts. The cure for St. Clair's scepticism would have been an earnest and impartial study
of the arguments, and the evidence, for and against
Christianity. We say for and *against*, because a man
who has once doubted will never be effectually convinced as long as he knows, or even suspects, that

* Chapter 27.

there is a side of the question which he has not examined. He who is afraid to do this is not a real believer, though he may think himself one.

The only remaining character on which we need dwell is Topsy. She is, perhaps, the most popular of all Mrs. Stowe's *dramatis personæ*, probably because she is the most original. Nature intended her to be intelligent and affectionate, but she has grown up to girlhood without having ever received instruction or experienced kindness. So far, perhaps, she does not differ much from many of the outcast children that are thrown up from time to time in our police courts. But she is marked by a peculiarity not to be found in Europe, unless it be among the Cagots, if any are left, of the South of France, the feeling that she belongs to a degraded caste. " There can't nobody love niggers, and niggers can't do nothing," is the creed which a life of twelve years in New Orleans has taught her. Though she cannot be loved, however, she can be admired and feared. All the children are delighted by her drollery, grimace, and mimicry ; and the elder members of the servants' hall find that whoever casts any indignity upon Topsy, is sure to meet with some inconvenient accident shortly after. Her great pride is in her wickedness.

" ' Lor, you niggers,' she says to her young admirers,
" ' does you know you's all sinners ? Well you is —
" ' every body is: white folk is sinners too — Miss
" ' Feely says so; but I spects niggers is the biggest
" ' ones : but Lor ye an't any on you up to me. I's
" ' so awfully wicked, there can't nobody do nothing
" ' with me. I spects I's the wickedest critter in the
" ' world.' And Topsy would cut a somersault and
" come up brisk and shining, and evidently plume
" herself on the distinction."

The way in which this hardened nature, after hav-

E

ing resisted the cold kindness of Ophelia, is at once
subdued and softened by the compassion and love of
Eva, deserves the admiration which it has received.

The last source, that occurs to us, of Uncle Tom's
popularity in England, is the state of the English and
American law as to literary property. Each country
refuses copyright to the citizens of the other. The
necessary consequence is, that an English work which
has acquired celebrity enough to be reprinted in
America, reappears there in a form so cheap, that an
enormous sale is ensured. More than 100,000 copies
of "Macaulay's History" were sold in America. The
English sale was very great, but we do not believe
that it exceeded 30,000. The same is the case with
English reprints of American works. "Uncle Tom"
costs probably eight shillings in America, and only
one here. The American sale was, as we have seen,
150,000 copies, while the English sale exceeded a
million.

Even the "White Slave," a disagreeable counterpart
of "Uncle Tom," in which the hero is in love with his
sister, and has his father for a rival, has had twice the
sale of the best of Walter Scott's or Miss Austen's
novels. It is as long as "Waverley" and sells for a
shilling. A remarkable result of this state of the
law in both countries is, that the popular literature of
America is English, and the popular literature of
England is American. Reprints of American works
of fiction, in which the matter of a large volume is
compressed into 400 duodecimo pages of small print
on bad, thin paper, cover the railway book stalls, and
filter from thence into the farmhouses and the back
rooms of the village shops. "Uncle Tom," "The
Wide Wide World," "Queechy," and "The White
Slave," form now the staple of the reading of the
middle classes.

The "Key to Uncle Tom's Cabin" is too long. The portion of it which shows that American slavery and the American slave trade can produce real events similar to those related in "Uncle Tom," was scarcely necessary. Such events are, as we have already remarked, the inevitable incidents to the system, nor is the production of a real counterpart for every story in "Uncle Tom" a complete defence of Mrs. Stowe against the charge of misrepresentation.

With respect to the internal slave trade of America, we do not believe misrepresentation to be possible. Every part of it is so utterly hateful, that its horrors cannot be exaggerated. But with respect to the treatment of slaves by their owners, while employed in their houses or in their fields, we think it possible that "Uncle Tom" may produce a false impression, not by describing events that do not happen, but by leading us to think that they happen habitually. It is probable, we hope that it is true, that there are twenty Shelbys for one Legree. Evil affects the imagination so much more pungently, and dwells so much more in the memory, than good, that if we run through a list of the railway accidents of a year, we are inclined for an instant to suppose railways to be the most dangerous means of travelling, instead of being, as they are, the safest. So after reading Mrs. Stowe, we forget the Shelbys, and remember only the Legrees. If Mrs. Stowe be accused, as perhaps she may fairly be, of producing this false impression, she cannot defend herself by proving, as she does triumphantly, that Legrees exist.

The great value of the "Key" consists in the specimens which it gives of the legislation of the Slave States, and of the arguments by which it is defended. One of the laws common to all the Slave States is the refusal to admit the testimony of a coloured person against a white. Such a law obviously deprives the whole coloured race of the protection, such as it is, which any other laws affect to give to them. The deliberate, intentional killing of a slave is now, by the laws of every state, murder. But a white may perpetrate it in the presence of hundreds. Hundreds of witnesses may be ready to prove it by direct evidence. They saw him take aim, fire, and the negro fall dead. The Court cannot hear them. Hundreds may be ready to prove it by circumstantial evidence. They heard him threaten to shoot the negro; they saw him load the gun, and go towards the field; they heard the explosion, they saw him return, and they heard him boast that he had shot Pompey. The Court cannot hear them. It can listen only to a white constable, who says that, "in consequence of something which was told to him," he went to a certain field, and there found the body of a negro with a wound in the breast; and the evidence of a white surgeon, who opened the body, and found the heart perforated by a bullet.

On such testimony alone, of course, no man can be convicted. A deed done in the face of day, in the presence of crowds, of which every detail is notorious, is to the Court, and to the Court alone, a mysterious event: perhaps a murder, perhaps a quarrel, perhaps a suicide, respecting which every attempt to obtain evidence or explanation has failed.

Mrs. Stowe has quoted the following passage from a speech of a Georgian clergyman, the Rev. Dr. Few, at a conference of the Methodist Church in which it was proposed to admit the testimony of coloured persons against whites in ecclesiastical matters: —

"Look at it! What do you declare to us, in tak-
"ing this course! Why, simply, as much as to say,

" ' We cannot sustain you in the condition which you
" cannot avoid ! ' We cannot sustain you in the ne-
" cessary conditions of slave holding ; one of its neces-
" sary conditions being the rejection of negro testi-
" mony ! If it is not sinful to hold slaves, under all
" circumstances, it is not sinful to hold them on the
" only condition, and under the only circumstances
" under which they can be held. The rejection of
" negro testimony is one of the necessary circumstances
" under which slave holding can exist ; indeed, it is ut-
" terly impossible for it to exist without it ; therefore,
" it is not sinful to hold slaves in the condition, and
" under the circumstances which they are held in the
" South, inasmuch as they can be held under no other
" circumstances . . . . If you believe that slave holding
" is necessarily sinful, come out with the abolitionists
" and honestly say so. If you believe that slave holding
" is necessarily sinful, you believe we are necessarily
" sinners ; and, if so, come out and honestly declare it,
" and let us leave you . . . . We want to know, dis-
" tinctly, precisely, and honestly, the position which
" you take. We cannot be tampered with by you any
" longer. We have had enough of it. We are tired
" of your sickly sympathies." *

But, after having thus carefully provided that even
the wilful deliberate murder of a negro shall not be
punishable unless it can be proved by the evidence of
a white, we are inclined to think that the Southern
legislators might have safely extended to their slaves
the protection which we give to horses, cattle, and
dogs. The grounds on which they have thought fit
to refuse to do so are well stated in the following
judgment of Chief Justice Ruffin, of North Carolina.
The question before him was, whether a person

* Key, book iv. chap. 1.
E 3

who had hired a slave could be indicted for inflicting
on that slave a punishment which was admitted to
have been "cruel, unwarrantable, and dispropor-
tioned to the offence."

"The question," says the Chief Justice, "has been
"assimilated at the bar to the other domestic rela-
"tions; and arguments drawn from the well estab-
"lished principles which confer and restrain the au-
"thority of the parent over the child, the tutor over
"the pupil, the master over the apprentice, have been
"pressed on us."

"The Court does not recognise that application:
"there is no likeness between the cases,—they are in
"opposition to each other; there is an impassable gulf
"between them. The difference is that which exists
"between freedom and slavery, and a greater cannot be
"imagined. In the one, the end in view is the happi-
"ness of the youth, born to equal rights with the
"governor on whom the duty devolves of training the
"youth to usefulness in a station which he is after-
"wards to assume among free men. To such an end,
"and with such an object, moral and intellectual in-
"struction seems the natural means; and, for the most
"part, they are found to suffice. Moderate force is
"superadded only to make the others effectual. If
"that fail, it is better to leave the party to his own
"headstrong passions, and the ultimate correction of
"the law, than to allow it to be immoderately inflicted
"by a private person."

"With slavery it is otherwise. The *end* is the
"profit of the master, his security, and the public
"safety: the subject is one doomed in his own person
"and in his posterity, to live without knowledge, and
"without the capacity to make anything his own, and
"to toil that another may reap the fruits. What moral
"considerations can be addressed to such a being

" to convince him, which it is impossible but that the
" most stupid must feel can never be true, that he is
" thus to labour upon a principle of natural duty, or
" for the sake of his own personal happiness ? Such
" services can be expected only from one who has no
" will of his own, who surrenders his will in implicit
" obedience to that of another. Such obedience is the
" consequence only of unlimited authority over the
" body. There is nothing else that can operate to pro-
" duce the effect. The power of the master must be ab-
" solute to render the submission of the slave perfect."

" I confess the harshness of this proposition. As a
" principle of moral right every man in his retirement
" must reprobate it. But, in the present state of
" things it must be so: there is no remedy. This dis-
" cipline belongs to the state of slavery. They cannot
" be disunited without abrogating the rights of the
" master, and absolving the slave from his subjection.
" It constitutes the curse of slavery to both the bond
" and the free portions of our community. It is in-
" herent in the relations of master and slave. In the
" abstract it may well be asked *what* powers of the
" master accord with right. The answer will probably
" sweep away all of them. But we cannot look at the
" matter in that light. We are forbidden to enter
" upon a train of general reasoning on the subject.
" We cannot allow the rights of the master to be
" brought into discussion in Courts of Justice. The
" slave, to remain a slave, must be made sensible that
" there is no appeal from his master: that the master's
" power is in no instance usurped, but is conferred by
" the law of man, at least, if not by the law of God."

" Judgment entered for the defendant."*

We join in Mrs. Stowe's admiration " of the

* Key, book ii. chap. 2.

" unflinching calmness, with which a man, evidently
" of humane, honourable feelings, walks through the
" most terrible results and conclusions in obedience to
" legal truth." Chief Justice Ruffin's exposition of the
law of North Carolina is, we have no doubt, accurate.
His defence of that law, as necessarily incidental to
the status of slavery, is bold and masterly; but it
does not convince us.   We do not believe that if the
" cruel, unwarrantable, and disproportionate punishment " of the slave were an indictable offence, a
master would run much chance of conviction by a
Carolina jury forbidden to receive negro evidence.
While the laws respecting such evidence remain unaltered, it seems to us unimportant what amount of
protection is pretended to be given to the slave, or
what amount of restraint is pretended to be imposed
on the master.

Mrs. Stowe goes on to quote a work by the Rev.
James Smylie, an eminent member of the Southern
Presbyterian Church, in defence of the laws prohibit-
ing the teaching slaves to read, — " Laws," says Mr.
Smylie, " meeting the approbation of the religious
" part of the reflecting community."

These laws, however, we can understand.   We are
not surprised that slave owners, living among enemies,
wish to deprive those enemies of the means of combination afforded by a written language.   We are
not surprised at their telling the slave that, while he
lives, there is no appeal for him against his master;
and that even his death under his master's hand is
not punishable, unless it can be proved that the
master's intention was to kill, — not merely to torture.   We are not surprised at their attempt, indirectly, to deprive the slave of the legal protection
against wilful murder, which shame forces them to
pretend to provide for him.

We see why, in every Slave State, the crime of a slave is punished far more severely than that of a free man.   The slave is already in a situation worse than any to which a free man can be reduced by punishment, short of perpetual imprisonment or death. Sufferings and degradations, from which a free man would escape by suicide, are the ordinary incidents to his status.   Habit prevents their having any terrors for him.   The only resources left to the law are torture, mutilation, and death.

We can understand the motive for enacting, in North Carolina, the law which justified the following proclamation, extracted by Mrs. Stowe from the " Wilmington Journal" of Dec. 13. 1850:—

" Whereas complaint has been made before us by Guilford Horn, that his slave Harry hath absented himself from his master's service, and is supposed to be lurking about in this county.   We do hereby, by virtue of the Act of Assembly in such cases made and provided, declare that if the said slave Harry doth not return home immediately, any person or persons may kill and destroy the said slave by such means as he or they may think fit, without impeachment of any offence for so doing.

" Given under our hands and seals this 29th June, 1850.

" J. T. MILLER, J. P.

" W. C. BETTENCOURT, J. P." *

We can understand, too, the motive for the supplementary law of that State, which enacts that when a runaway slave has been killed, in obedience to such a proclamation, his value shall be assessed by a jury,

* Key, p. 200.

and two-thirds of that value paid out of the public
treasury to the master—a law which accounts for the
following advertisement, published by the aforesaid
Guilford Horn : —

" One hundred and twenty-five dollars will be paid
for the delivery of the said Harry to me at Tosnott
Depôt, Edgecombe County ; *or one hundred and fifty
dollars will be given for his head.* He has a free
mulatto wife, lately removed to Wilmington, with
whom he will likely be lurking.   Masters of vessels
are cautioned against harbouring him, as the full
penalty of the law will be exacted."

Harry's head represented two-thirds of the value
which a jury might assess for his whole person.
Harry, alive, would probably have again run away
to his wife.   It was worth Mr. Horn's while to offer
a bribe of twenty-five dollars additional to Harry's
captors, if they would have the kindness to kill him,
instead of bringing him to Tosnott Depôt.

All this legislation has an intelligible object, and
pursues it by intelligible means.   But there are other
slave laws which, perhaps from our ignorance of the
circumstances which render them necessary, look, to
European eyes, like wanton cruelty.

The Americans probably think themselves more
civilised than the most barbarous of the inhabitants
of Europe, the Russians.   The great mitigation of
the slavery of Russia is the permission given by the
master to his serf to work, to trade, and to acquire
property for himself, paying to his master a rent,
called an obroc.   It is an arrangement eminently
useful to both parties and also to the country.   There
are considerable merchants, bankers, and tradesmen
who are slaves, whose services are valuable to the
public, and whose obroc forms the greater part of
their master's income.

Such contracts under the laws of the Slave States are not merely void, they are offences — for which the master is fined, the slave punished, and what he calls his property is confiscated.

Thus the law of Mississippi imposes a fine on a master convicted of permitting his slave to cultivate cotton for his own use, or of permitting him to keep stock of any description, or of licensing him to go at large and trade as a freeman. In North Carolina, the offence is committed by merely allowing the slave to go at large as a freeman, allowing him to trade is not essential. The allowing him to hire himself out for his own benefit is punished in Georgia by a fine on the master of thirty dollars a week. Of course the slave convicted of having been allowed to grow cotton, or convicted of having been allowed to keep stock, or convicted of having been allowed to go at large, or convicted of having been allowed to hire himself out, is punished separately.*

One of the safest modes of extinguishing slavery is gradual emancipation. It was thus that it disappeared in England. It is also the best palliative of existing slavery. It holds out a reward for good conduct, the only permanent reward that can be held out to a slave. It substitutes hope for fear.

In South Carolina, Georgia, Alabama, and Mississippi, it is an offence. It can indeed be effected, as everything can be effected, by an Act of the Legislature, that is to say, by a law passed for the purpose of emancipating a given slave — but every attempt to do it privately, by the mere will of the master, is punished, as respects the emancipator by a heavy fine, as respects the slave by his being sold by auction for the benefit of the State.

* Key, chap. 13.

The working of the law may be brought practically before the reader by the following case.

A man named Elisha Brazaelle, a planter in Jefferson County, Mississippi, was nursed during a long illness by a young coloured slave girl. Feeling that he owed to her his life, he rewarded her by taking her to Ohio, a Free State, and educating her there. She grew up an intelligent accomplished woman, and he married her, having previously executed a deed for her emancipation, which was recorded in the States both of Ohio and of Mississippi. He had by her a son, named James Monroe Brazaelle, who, from his parentage, must have been nearly white. The family lived for many years in Mississippi, and Elisha Brazaelle died there, having by his will, which recited and confirmed the deed of emancipation, provided for his widow, and devised all the rest of his property to his son.

Some poor and distant relations in North Carolina heard of the death, and filed a bill in the Court of Equity in Mississippi, claiming the property, and, as part of the property, claiming also the widow and son, of the testator. The case is reported in Howard's Mississippi Reports, vol. ii. p. 837.

We copy from Mrs. Stowe, an extract from the judgment of the Chief Justice, one Sharkey.

"To give validity," says the Judge, "to the deed " of emancipation would be a violation of the declared " policy, and contrary to a positive law, of the State."

" The policy of a State is indicated by the general " course of legislation on a given subject; and we find " that free negroes are deemed offensive, because they " are not permitted to emigrate to, or remain in, the " State. They are allowed few privileges, and subject " to heavy penalties for offences. They are required to " leave the State within thirty days after notice, and in

" the meantime to give security for good behaviour;
" and those of them who can lawfully remain must re-
" gister and carry with them their certificates, or they
" may be committed to jail. It would also violate a
" positive law, passed by the Legislature, expressly to
" maintain this settled policy, and to prevent emanci-
" pation. No owner can emancipate his slave, but by
" deed or will properly attested, or acknowledged in
" Court, and proof to the Legislature that such slave
" has performed some meritorious act for the benefit
" of the master, or some distinguished service for the
" State; and the deed or will can have no validity
" until ratified by a special Act of the Legislature.
" It is believed that this law and policy are too
" essentially important to the interests of our citizens
" to permit them to be evaded."

  " The state of the case shows conclusively that the
" emancipation *had its origin in an offence against*
" *morality, pernicious and detestable as an example. —*
" But above all, it seems to have been planned and
" executed with a fixed design to evade the rigour of
" the laws of this State. The acts of the party in
" going to Ohio with the slave, and there executing the
" deed, and his immediate return to this State, point,
" with unerring certainty, to his purpose and object.
" The laws of this State cannot be thus defrauded of
" their operation by one of our own citizens. If we
" could have any doubts about the principle, the case
" reported in 1 Randolph, 15. would remove them."

  " As we think the validity of the deed must depend
" upon the laws of this State, it becomes unnecessary
" to inquire whether it could have any force by the
" laws of Ohio. If it were even valid there, it can have
" no force here. The consequence is, that the negroes,
" John Monroe Brazaelle and his mother, are still
" slaves, and a part of the estate of Elisha Brazaelle.

" They have not acquired a right to their freedom un-
" der the will; for, even if the clause in the will were
" sufficient for that purpose, their emancipation has not
" been consummated by an Act of the Legislature."

" John Monroe Brazaelle, being a slave, cannot
" take the property as devisee; and I apprehend it is
" equally clear that it cannot be held in trust for
" him. (4 Desans. Rep. 266.) Independent of the
" principles laid down in adjudicated cases, our statute
" law prohibits slaves from owning certain kinds of
" property; and it may be inferred that the Legislature
" supposed they were extending the Act as far as it
" could be necessary to exclude them from owning *any*
" property, as the prohibition includes that kind of
" property which they would most likely be permitted
" to own without any interruption, to wit, hogs, horses,
" cattle, &c. &c. They cannot be prohibited from hold-
" ing such property, in consequence of its being of a
" dangerous or offensive character, but because it was
" deemed impolitic for them to hold property of *any*
" description. It follows, therefore, that Elisha Bra-
" zaelle's heirs are entitled to the property." *

The property being, the estate, the slaves, and,
among the slaves, the widow and son and devisee of
the testator, educated in affluence, freedom, and refinement, and now slaves for ever.

When we look back at this frightful code we feel
the force of Mrs. Stowe's remark, that it is not by in-
sulated attempts to better the condition of the slaves
on any given plantation, but by repealing the local
legislation of the Slave States, that permanent or
general improvement is to be effected. While the
laws remain unaltered nothing can be done.

Let us suppose the case of a Georgian, who suc-

* Key, p. 275.

ceeds, when he comes of age, to a property consisting
of 2000 acres of land, with the necessary buildings
and live and dead stock, including in the live stock
500 slaves.   Let him be convinced of the wickedness
of slaveholding, and of the still greater wickedness of
slave trading, and resolved at least to free his own
soul from the crime.

The obvious course is to do as George Shelby does
in " Uncle Tom," to emancipate his slaves, and retain them as free labourers on wages.

" This is illegal : " in the words of Chief Justice
Sharkey, " it is an offence against morality, perni-
" cious and detestable as an example."   The master
who is guilty of emancipating is fined 1000 dollars.
The slave who is convicted of having been emancipated is to be sold by public outcry for the benefit of
the State.

If he cannot emancipate his slaves in Georgia, he
may take them to a Free State and set them free
there.   To do so of course is utter ruin, — the land
without the slaves is valueless ; but he prefers ruin
to self-reproach.

But not one of them can read or write — they can
do nothing but grow cotton and pick it.   Five hundred such helpless beings cast adrift in a Free State,
in which a negro is an object of contempt and disgust, would starve.   He must attempt to educate
and prepare them for freedom, and begins by having
them taught to read.

It is illegal ; it subjects him to a fine of thirty dollars for each offence, that is to say, for each time
that each slave is instructed, and subjects his coloured teachers male and female to imprisonment
and thirty-nine lashes.

He submits then to retain them on his estate, but
resolves that at least none shall be sold off.   He is

forced to be a slave holder, but thanks God that he cannot be forced to be a slave trader.

But the laws of population pursue their irresistible course. In a state of society in which the expense of a child falls not on the parents, but on their master, there can be no preventive check. In a plantation in which the negroes are not overworked or underfed, there can be no physical check. Nothing but the most grinding oppression, or the disproportion between the sexes incident to a country that imports slaves, can prevent a slave population from doubling every twenty-five years. In fact, notwithstanding much oppression, the slave population of the United States does double in a less period than every twenty-five years.

In a few years, therefore, the 500 slaves with whom our planter began have increased to 750 — in a few years more they will be 1000 — the 2000 acres cannot employ them : they soon will not be able to feed them.

He attempts to relieve himself by letting those who think that they can shift for themselves go at large. It is illegal — as before, he is fined and the slave is punished.

He thinks that he may be able to turn to account some of the outlying portions of his estate, and to diminish the burden of its excessive population, by letting his slaves cultivate it for their own benefit, and support themselves by keeping stock on it.

It is illegal—he is fined, the slave is punished, and the stock is confiscated and sold for the benefit of the State and of the informer.

By the time he is between sixty and seventy, his slaves have increased from 500 to 1500. His whole land is devoted to their support and is insufficient.

He must either starve them or sell them.

And these are the laws of a country that calls itself free !

We have said that such oppression is not to be found in Naples, in Turkey, or in Russia. We do not believe that such oppression is to be found in any other part of the world, civilised or uncivilised. We do not believe that such oppression ever existed before. The slavery of Greece as well as that of Rome was atrocious. We have no doubt that it was far more cruel, — using the word "cruel" to signify the infliction of torture or death,—than that of America. It was characterised by the indifference to human suffering which belongs to Paganism. But its oppression was less degrading, less systematic, less unrelenting. It deprived the slave of liberty, but it left him hope. It gave to the master full power to ill-treat his slaves, but it also gave to him full power to benefit them. The slave might be instructed, he might have a sort of property, he might have his freedom.

"Et spes libertatis erat, et cura peculi."

Republican America has elaborated a tyranny such as no democracy, no aristocracy, no monarchy, no despotism, ever perpetrated, or, as far as we know, ever imagined.

But how is the alteration of these laws to be effected ?

With few, we fear very few, exceptions, the minds of all classes in the Slave States seem, on the subject of slavery, to be perverted. The higher classes, the workers and breeders of slaves, are blinded by their interests. The lower classes, the "poor white trash," whom the want of education, the want of employment, and the disgracefulness of labour, have degraded below the level of the lowest European proletaires, are

F

ferocious partisans of every law which keeps another
class below them. It is some consolation in their
misery, that they have a right to trample on the majority of their fellow citizens. They constitute the
ferocious mob which the slave owners and slave
traders let loose on all who are suspected of being
abolitionists.

As for the clergy, the most powerful body in the
United States, the body through whose influence
slavery was gradually extinguished in Europe, they
are utterly corrupted by their subserviency to their
employers. Some of them are members of the vigilance committees, who form an Inquisition, differing
from that of Rome only in that it persecutes abolitionists instead of heretics, and that its proceedings
are illegal, and consequently that it employs mobs for
its instruments instead of officials. All of them have
prostituted their knowledge, and the respect due to
their functions, by indiscriminate defence, not only of
slavery, but of the very laws which, as we have seen,
while they last, render slavery irremediable.

There is not a Slave State in which an attempt to
repeal these laws would not be worse than fruitless,
in which it would not expose its proposers, and all
who were suspected of approving the proposal, to
insults, assaults, and perhaps death. Such a repeal
must be imposed from without; there is no tendency
towards it within. The slavery of the British colonies
was softened, and finally abolished, by the central
Government. If it had been left to the local legislatures, it would have been still existing, probably
unmitigated, perhaps exasperated. The United States
possess a central authority, which has power to declare
all these laws unconstitutional and void; which can
repeal them and prohibit their reenactment; but such
enactments could be made binding on all the States

only by being introduced as amendments into the Constitution. The Constitution of the United States, as is generally the case with the constitutions of nations which have created them *de novo*, instead of gradually evolving them, can be altered only by a slow and difficult process. Congress cannot make amendments in it without the consent of two-thirds of both houses, and cannot call a convention to make them without the concurrence of the legislatures of two-thirds of the States, and when made they require ratification by three-fourths of the States.

The Free States are now sixteen, the Slave States fifteen. To obtain the requisite majority of three-fourths, six of the Slave States must join the Free States. We do not believe that this is to be hoped for now. If, under the operation of the Nebraska and Kansas Act, two or three more Slave States are added to the Union, it will become obviously impossible.

That Act, however, is not part of the Constitution. Congress, by a simple majority, can repeal it, and arrest the territorial progress of slavery.

It can also repeal the Fugitive Slave Act, and relieve the Northerns from the hateful liability to become slave hunters for the Southerns.

But it can do no more.

Beyond the repeal of these Acts, what can an American statesman, anxious to free his country from this intolerable load of misery and crime effect?

Nothing.

He may indulge the hope that the ameliorating influence of knowledge and religion will induce the inhabitants of the Southern States themselves to amend gradually their atrocious slave codes. He may console himself with such a hope. We should be sorry to deprive him of it, but we do not share it. Public opinion in the Slave States instead of improving is deteriorating. There are no instruments by which it can be enlightened or shamed. The press, the pulpit, the legislative bodies are silenced. Any man "tainted," to use the language of a Southern Presbyterian clergyman, "with the blood-hound prin-"ciples of abolition," * or even suspected of being so tainted, is ruined, outraged, and exiled, if he is allowed to live.†

That Providence will, in its own way and in its own time, work out a cure, we believe; because we believe improvement, progressive, though always slow and often interrupted, to be among the laws by which this earth is governed. But we do not venture to hope that we, or our sons, or our grandsons, will see American slavery extirpated, or even materially mitigated.

　　* Key, p. 492.　　　　　　　† See Note II.

NOTE I., p. 27.

The following story, which we take from an American paper of July, 1855, illustrates the remarks in the text.

" A Mr. Pardon Davis, of Marquette County, in the State of Wisconsin, was temporarily resident at Tensas, in Louisiana, near which was a plantation, the scene of horrible cruelties.   Some negroes escaped from it, took refuge in his wood-yard, were concealed by him, and sent in a canoe across the river.   A negro-hunter discovered their trail, hunted them for forty miles, overtook them, and gave them to his dogs to be worried, until at last they confessed whence they came and who had assisted them.   For this crime Mr. Davis was sentenced to twenty years' imprisonment in the State prison of Louisiana, and is now at Baton Rouge undergoing his punishment.

" The following passages are extracted from a letter, which he wrote before his trial, to the Baptist community of which he is a member.

" ' I ask my brethren and sisters, in the fear of God, if a man should come to you, presenting a lacerated back, exposed to the rays of a southern summer's sun for want of a shirt, feet bleeding from having been torn by snags and briars, hungry and faint, whose crime was that he failed, after straining every nerve, to perform the labour appointed him—I ask, would you—could you—turn him away without assisting him?   No, brethren, I think I know you too well — I think you would hand up a loaf of bread, part with some of your surplus clothing, or, if you had no surplus, buy some, as I did — help them across the river, point them to the star of Liberty, and bid them God speed.

" ' And now what more can I say?   Have I done wrong? Have I done more than any *man* ought to do?   Dear brethren, I leave you to judge; I am willing to be governed by your decision.   I wait with the greatest anxiety to hear from you, to know whether I shall receive your sympathies and prayers, or whether I have done wrong and am considered a heathen. If the former, I can bear my affliction with fortitude; but if the latter, I feel that my life hangs by a slender thread — that my days are numbered. In the meantime, brethren, pray for me; sisters, remember me in your prayers.

"'I must cease, for the last paper in my possession is nearly covered over. And now, my brethren, when you meet to pray for heathen lands, remember, O! remember our own country. Watch over the declining steps of my parents; 'tis the greatest boon I can ask, for I fear that this intelligence will bring the grey hairs of loving father and affectionate mother to the grave. Comfort them with the thought that we may meet in heaven.'"

Note II., p. 68.

Even in Virginia, once the most civilised of the States, to speak, though in another State, against slavery is punished by exile.

This crime was committed by a Mr. Underwood, a Virginian, on the 26th of June, 1856. We copy a letter to him from his wife, warning him of what was to come, and also the sentence inflicted on him by a self-constituted tribunal.

"June 23rd, 1856.
"My Dear John C.,
    "A friend communicated to me yesterday that there existed the greatest excitement and indignation against you for making, as reported in *The Herald*, an anti-slavery speech.   —— told our friend, they were watching at Piedmont on Saturday for your arrival, and he had no doubt

if you had come that day, you would have met with personal violence.   At Markham Station the leaders say they go for giving you notice, and a reasonable time to wind up your business and leave the State.   I send this morning to Alexandria to mail this letter at that place, and telegraph to you to remain in New York till you receive it.   I know not what to advise.   I am afraid the excitement will meet you if you come.   You know I am a Jackson, and I could not have Jackson blood in my veins without resisting till the last drop is shed in defence of life and liberty; but I do not believe in courting mob law or martyrdom.   I feel greatly troubled at this state of things, and fear if your speech can be obtained it will exasperate the people here greatly.   I hope you will be prudent; remain awhile in New York. Write immediately, and tell me what to do on the farm, and I will try to have your wishes carried out as nearly as I can.

" With sorrow and much love, I remain, as ever,

" Your devoted wife,

" M. G. UNDERWOOD."

FROM " THE VIRGINIA SENTINEL," JUNE 27TH, 1856.

" At a large and respectable meeting held at Piedmont Station, on the 26th instant, for the purpose of expressing their sentiments in relation to the course pursued by John C. Underwood, of Clarke County, and George Rye, of Shenandoah, at the Black Republican Convention, recently held at Philadelphia —

" Resolved, That a committee be appointed to wait upon Mr. Underwood, to inform him of the just feelings of indignation created by his course in the Convention, together with his former (reputed) course in regard to the institution of slavery, and that they deem it just and advisable that he should leave the State as speedily as he can find it in his power so to do.

" Resolved, That the Alexandria *Gazette*, Alexandria

Sentinel, Virginia papers generally, the *National Intelligencer,* and Baltimore *Sun,* are requested to insert the above as an act of justice to the citizens of our State.

" EDWIN S. ASHBY, Secretary.
" ROBERT SINGLETON, Chairman."

Mr. Sumner's speech will be made more intelligible to an English reader by the following extract from a sermon preached by the Rev. Dudley Tyng in Philadelphia, on the 29th June, 1856:—

" On the 30th of May, 1854, the Territory of Kansas was thrown open to settlers by act of Congress, and the privilege of determining the character of its institutions accorded to those who should become residents of its soil. Attracted by this opening for industry and enterprise, large numbers of persons from all sections of the country emigrated to the Territory, and soon made its prairies to smile with cultivation, and dotted its surface with towns and villages. Never country opened with brighter prospects. But how soon was the bright morn overcast! On the 29th of November, 1854, the infant Territory was to elect a Delegate to appear and speak in its behalf in the National Congress. On that day more than one thousand armed men from an adjoining State invaded the Territory, drove judges and legal voters from the polls, and, by fraudulent ballots, elected a man of their own. On the 30th of March, 1855, the inhabitants of Kansas were to have elected their Territorial Legislature. More than four thousand armed men from the same State again invaded the Territory, took possession of the polls and elected their own candidates, some of them residents of their own State. The recent investigations of the Congressional Committee have proved that of five thousand five hundred votes cast on that day, less than one thousand were of actual residents of the Territory.

Surely it was bad enough to see a Legislature imposed on them by force and fraud. But what sort of laws did they pass? Hear and ask yourselves whether

we live in the Nineteenth Century, and in a free and
Christian Republic.   They re-enacted in a mass all
the slave laws of Missouri, merely adding that wherever the word 'State' occurs in them it shall be
construed to mean 'Territory.'   They made non-
admission of the right to hold slaves in the Territory
a disqualification for sitting as Juror.   They enacted
that to say that persons have not a right to hold
slaves in that Territory should be punished with two
years' imprisonment at hard labour; that writing, printing, or circulating anything against slavery should
be punished with five years' imprisonment at hard
labour; that the harbouring of fugitive slaves should
be punished with five years' imprisonment at hard
labour; that assisting slaves to escape from any
Territory, and take refuge in that Territory, should
be punished with *death;* that the printing or circulation of publications calculated to incite slaves to
insurrection should be punished with *death;* to secure
these laws perpetuity, they enacted that all who do
not swear to support the Fugitive Slave law should
be disqualified as voters, but that any one might vote
who will pay one dollar and swear to uphold the
Fugitive Slave law and the Nebraska bill.   And, still
further to guard against all contingencies, they appointed non-residents to town and county offices for
six years ahead."

" Thus, by one stroke of combined fraud and force,
the great questions of social rights, whose settlement
had been pledged to the citizens themselves, were decided by an invading army, whose agents establish
Slavery against the wishes of the people, disfranchise
all who oppose it, open the polls to all pro-slavery
non-residents, and shut up all who speak, write,
print, or circulate anything against it with long imprisonment at hard labour.   What has become of

the rights of American citizens? Talk of obedience to law! Would you, would any American, obey such laws so imposed? Where were the spirit of our Revolutionary fathers if such oppression could be submitted to? Where is our Republican Government if such rights can be taken away?"

"But what was done in opposition? There was no armed resistance, no collision with assumed authority. The people of Kansas simply denied the legality of the enactments and the obligation of obedience, and then, falling back on inherent rights, went through the preliminaries of a State organisation, and applied to Congress for relief. That relief has not been yet afforded. And what has since transpired? A third, fourth and fifth armed invasion has taken place, each with increased aggravation of outrage. Pillage, and plunder, and murder, have increased from day to day. Large bodies of armed men from distant and adjoining States are in the Territory, with no attempt at becoming settlers, without means of honest support, living by the pillage of those who differ from themselves in sentiment, and perpetrating cruelties unknown even in war. Government troops have been used to overawe all attempts at resistance, and moved about so as to expose unprotected towns to violence. A fourfold process of oppression has been used to ruin and drive out those whose only crime is the claiming of rights guaranteed to them by the very law which invited them to Kansas. First, innumerable indictments for imaginary crimes are made out by a corrupt judiciary against all Free State men of influence, while the worst of crimes, by men of opposite politics, have gone unnoticed. Secondly, armed hordes of ruffians, under pretence of maintaining 'law and order,' patrol the country, committing all the outrages which have

been described. Thirdly, the United States dra-
goons are made use of by the local authorities to
suppress any risings for self-defence, and kept out of
the way when attacks are to be made. And, lastly,
'Vigilance Committees' are appointed to drive off,
with threats of 'Lynch law,' all those who, by the
other methods, have not been subdued. All this has
been going on for months. And recent accounts an-
nounce that the sufferers themselves are driven by
desperation to armed defence, and the hostile bands
are now watching each other, and meeting in deadly
conflict. Civil war is begun."

A SPEECH

DELIVERED BY

THE HON. CHARLES SUMNER,

IN THE

SENATE OF THE UNITED STATES,

On the 19*th and* 20*th May,* 1856.

Mr. PRESIDENT:

You are now called to redress a great transgression. Seldom in the history of nations has such a question been presented. Tariffs, army bills, navy bills, land bills, are important, and justly occupy your care; but these all belong to the course of ordinary legislation. As means and instruments only, they are necessarily subordinate to the conservation of Government itself. Grant them or deny them, in greater or less degree, and you will inflict no shock; the machinery of Government will continue to move; the State will not cease to exist. Far otherwise is it with the eminent question now before you, involving, as it does, Liberty in a broad Territory, and also involving the peace of the whole country with our good name in history for evermore.

Take down your map, sir, and you will find that the Territory of Kansas, more than any other region, occupies the middle spot of North America, equally distant from the Atlantic on the east, and the Pacific on the west; from the frozen waters of Hudson's Bay on the north, and the tepid Gulf Stream on the south, constituting the precise territorial centre of the whole vast Continent. To such advantages of situation, on the very highway between two oceans, are added a soil of unsurpassed richness, and a fascinating, undulating beauty of surface, with a health-giving climate, calculated to nurture a powerful and generous people, worthy to be a central pivot of American Institutions. A few short months only have passed since this spacious mediterranean country was open only to the savage, who ran wild in its woods and prairies; and now it has already drawn to its bosom a population of freemen larger than Athens crowded within her historic gates, when her sons, under Miltiades, won Liberty for mankind on the field of Marathon; more than Sparta contained when she ruled Greece, and sent forth her devoted children, quickened by a mother's benediction, to return with their shields or on them; more than Rome gathered on her seven hills, when, under her kings, she commenced that sovereign sway, which afterwards embraced the whole earth; more than London held, when, on the fields of Crecy and Agincourt, the English banner was carried victoriously over the chivalrous hosts of France.

Against this Territory, thus fortunate in position and population, a Crime has been committed, which is without example in the records of the Past. Not in plundered provinces or in the cruelties of selfish governors will you find its parallel; and yet there is an ancient instance, which may show at least the path of justice. In the terrible impeachment by which the great Roman orator has blasted through all time the name of Verres, amidst charges of robbery and sacrilege, the enormity which most aroused the indignant voice of his accuser, and which still stands forth with strongest distinctness, arresting the sympathetic indignation of all who read the story, is, that away in Sicily he had scourged a citizen of Rome —that the cry "I am a Roman citizen" had been interposed in vain against the lash of the tyrant governor. Other charges were, that he had carried away productions of art, and that he had violated the sacred shrines. It was in the presence of the Roman Senate that this arraignment proceeded; in a temple of the Forum; amidst crowds, such as no orator had ever before drawn together, thronging the porticos and colonnades, even clinging to the house-tops and neighbouring slopes; and under the anxious gaze of witnesses summoned from the scene of crime. But an audience grander far, of higher dignity, of more various people and of wider intelligence — the countless multitude of succeeding generations, in every land, where eloquence has been studied, or where the Roman name has been recognised — has listened to the accusation, and throbbed with condemnation of the criminal. Sir, speaking in an age of light and in a land of constitutional liberty, where the safeguards of elections are justly placed among the highest triumphs of civilisation, I fearlessly assert that the wrongs of much abused Sicily, thus memorable in history, were small by the side of the wrongs of Kansas, where the very shrines of popular institutions, more sacred than any heathen altar, have been desecrated; where the ballot-box, more precious than any work, in ivory or marble, from the cunning hand of art, has been plundered; and where

the cry, " I am an American citizen," has been interposed in vain against outrage of every kind, even
upon life itself. Are you against sacrilege ? I present
it for your execration. Are you against robbery ? I
hold it up to your scorn. Are you for the protection
of American citizens ? I show you how their dearest
rights have been cloven down, while a Tyrannical
Usurpation has sought to instal itself on their very
necks!

But the wickedness which I now begin to expose
is immeasurably aggravated by the motive which
prompted it. Not in any common lust for power did
this uncommon tragedy have its origin. It is the
rape of a virgin Territory, compelling it to the hateful embrace of Slavery ; and it may be clearly traced
to a depraved longing for a new Slave State, the
hideous offspring of such a crime, in the hope of
adding to the power of Slavery in the National Government. Yes, Sir, when the whole world, alike
Christian and Turk, is rising up to condemn this
wrong, and to make it a hissing to the nations, here
in our Republic, *force*—aye, sir, FORCE—has been
openly employed in compelling Kansas to this pollution, and all for the sake of political power. There is
the simple fact, which you will vainly attempt to
deny, but which in itself presents an essential wickedness that makes other public crimes seem like public
virtues.

But this enormity, vast beyond comparison, swells
to dimensions of wickedness which the imagination
toils in vain to grasp, when it is understood, that for
this purpose are hazarded the horrors of intestine
feud, not only in this distant territory, but everywhere throughout the country. Already the muster
has begun. The strife is no longer local, but national.
Even now, while I speak, portents hang on all the

arches of the horizon, threatening to darken the broad land, which already yawns with the mutterings of civil war. The fury of the propagandists of Slavery, and the calm determination of their opponents, are now diffused from the distant territory over widespread communities, and the whole country, in all its extent—marshalling hostile divisions, and foreshadowing a strife, which, unless happily averted by the triumph of freedom, will become war—fratricidal, parricidal war—with an accumulated wickedness beyond the wickedness of any war in human annals; justly provoking the avenging judgment of Providence and the avenging pen of history, and constituting a strife, in the language of the ancient writer, more than *foreign*, more than *social*, more than *civil*; but something compounded of all these strifes, and in itself more than war; *sed potius commune quoddam ex omnibus, et plus quam bellum.*

Such is the crime which you are to judge. But the criminal also must be dragged into day, that you may see and measure the power by which all this wrong is sustained. From no common source could it proceed. In its perpetration, was needed a spirit of vaulting ambition which would hesitate at nothing; a hardihood of purpose which was insensible to the judgment of mankind; a madness for slavery which should disregard the Constitution, the laws, and all the great examples of our history; also a consciousness of power, such as comes from the habit of power; a combination of energies found only in a hundred arms directed by a hundred eyes; a control of Public Opinion, through venal pens and a prostituted press; an ability to subsidise crowds in every vocation of life—the politician with his local importance, the lawyer with his subtle tongue, and even the authority of the judge on the bench; and a familiar use of men in places high and low, so that none, from the President to the lowest border postmaster, should decline to be its tool; all these things and more were needed; and they were found in the Slave Power of our Republic. There, sir, stands the criminal—all unmasked before you—heartless, grasping, and tyrannical— with an audacity beyond that of Verres, a subtlety beyond that of Machiavel, a meanness beyond that of Bacon, and an ability beyond that of Hastings. Justice to Kansas can be secured only by the prostration of this influence; for this is the power behind— greater than any President—which succours and sustains the crime. Nay, the proceedings I now arraign derive their fearful consequence only from this connection.

In now opening this great matter, I am not insensible to the austere demands of the occasion; but the dependence of the crime against Kansas upon the Slave Power is so peculiar and important, that I trust to be pardoned while I impress it by an illustration, which to some may seem trivial. It is related in Northern mythology, that the god of Force, visiting an enchanted region, was challenged by his royal entertainer to what seemed a humble feat of strength — merely, sir, to lift a cat from the ground. The god smiled at the challenge, and, calmly placing his hand under the belly of the animal, with superhuman strength, strove, while the back of the feline monster arched far upwards, even beyond reach, and one paw actually forsook the earth, until at last the discomfited divinity desisted. But he was little surprised at his defeat, when he learned that this creature, which seemed to be a cat, and nothing more, was not merely a cat, but that it belonged to, and was a part of, the great Terrestrial Serpent, which, in its innumerable folds, encircled the whole globe. Even so the creature, whose paws are now fastened upon Kansas, whatever it may seem to be, constitutes in reality a part of the Slave Power, which, with loathsome folds, is now coiled about the whole land. Thus do I expose the extent of the present contest, where we encounter not merely local resistance, but also the unconquered sustaining arm behind. But out of the vastness of the crime attempted, with all its woe and shame, I derive a well-founded assurance of a commensurate vastness of effort against it, by the aroused masses of the country, determined not only to vindicate Right against Wrong, but to redeem the Republic from the thraldom of that Oligarchy, which prompts, directs, and concentrates, the distant wrong.

Such is the crime, and such the criminal, which it is my duty in this debate to expose, and, by the blessing of God, this duty shall be done completely to the end. But this will not be enough. The apologies, which, with strange hardihood, have been offered for the crime, must be torn away, so that it shall stand forth, without a single rag, or fig-leaf, to cover its vileness. And, finally, the true remedy must be shown. The subject is complex in its relations, as it is transcendent in importance; and yet, if I am honoured by your attention, I hope to exhibit it clearly in all its parts, while I conduct you to the inevitable conclusion, that Kansas must be admitted at once, with her present Constitution, as a State of this Union, and give a new star to the blue field of our national flag. And here I derive satisfaction from the thought that the cause is so strong in itself as to bear even the infirmities of its advocates; nor can it require anything beyond that simplicity of treatment and moderation of manner which I desire to cultivate. Its true character is such,

that, like Hercules, it will conquer just so soon as it
is recognised.

My task will be divided under three different
heads; *first*, THE CRIME AGAINST KANSAS, in its origin
and extent; *secondly*, THE APOLOGIES FOR THE CRIME;
and *thirdly*, THE TRUE REMEDY.

But, before entering upon the argument, I must
say something of a general character, particularly in
response to what has fallen from Senators who have
raised themselves to eminence on this floor in cham-
pionship of human wrongs; I mean the Senator from
South Carolina [Mr. BUTLER], and the Senator from
Illinois [Mr. DOUGLAS], who, though unlike as Don
Quixote and Sancho Panza, yet, like this couple, sally
forth together in the same adventure. I regret much
to miss the elder 'Senator from his seat; but the
cause, against which he has run a tilt, with such
activity of animosity, demands that the opportunity
of exposing him should not be lost; and it is for the
cause that I speak. The Senator from South Carolina
has read many books of chivalry, and believes himself
a chivalrous knight, with sentiments of honour and
courage. Of course he has chosen a mistress to whom
he has made his vows, and who, though ugly to others,
is always lovely to him; though polluted in the sight
of the world, is chaste in his sight—I mean the harlot,
Slavery. For her, his tongue is always profuse in
words. Let her be impeached in character, or any
proposition made to shut her out from the extension
of her wantonness, and no extravagance of manner
or hardihood of assertion is then too great for this
Senator. The frenzy of Don Quixote, in behalf of
his wench Dulcinea del Toboso, is all surpassed. The
asserted rights of Slavery, which shock equality of all

kinds, are cloaked by a fantastic claim of equality. If the Slave States cannot enjoy what, in mockery of the great fathers of the Republic, he misnames equality under the Constitution — in other words, the full power in the National Territories to compel fellow-men to unpaid toil, to separate husband and wife, and to sell little children at the auction block — then, sir, the chivalric Senator will conduct the State of South Carolina out of the Union! Heroic knight! Exalted Senator! A second Moses come for a second exodus!

But not content with this poor menace, which we have been twice told was "measured," the Senator, in the unrestrained chivalry of his nature, has undertaken to apply opprobrious words to those who differ from him on this floor. He calls them "sectional and fanatical;" and opposition to the usurpation in Kansas, he denounces as "an uncalculating fanaticism." To be sure, these charges lack all grace of originality, and all sentiment of truth; but the adventurous Senator does not hesitate. He is the uncompromising, unblushing representative on this floor of a flagrant *sectionalism*, which now domineers over the Republic; and yet with a ludicrous ignorance of his own position—unable to see himself as others see him — or with an effrontery which even his white head ought not to protect from rebuke, he applies to those here who resist his *sectionalism* the very epithet which designates himself. The men who strive to bring back the Government to its original policy, when Freedom and not Slavery was national, while Slavery and not Freedom was sectional, he arraigns as *sectional*. This will not do. It involves too great a perversion of terms. I tell that Senator, that it is to himself, and to the "organisation" of which he is the "committed advocate," that this epithet belongs.

I now fasten it upon them. For myself, I care little
for names; but since the question has been raised
here, I affirm that the Republican party of the Union
is in no just sense *sectional*, but, more than any other
party, *national;* and that it now goes forth to dis-
lodge from the high places of the Government the
tyrannical sectionalism of which the Senator from
South Carolina is one of the maddest zealots.

To the charge of fanaticism I also reply. Sir,
fanaticism is found in an enthusiasm or exaggeration
of opinions, particularly on religious subjects; but
there may be a fanaticism for evil as well as for good.
Now, I will not deny that there are persons among
us loving Liberty too well for their personal good, in
a selfish generation. Such there may be, and, for
the sake of their example, would that there were
more! In calling them "fanatics" you cast contumely upon the noble army of martyrs, from the
earliest day down to this hour; upon the great tri-
bunes of human rights, by whom life, liberty, and
happiness, on earth, have been secured; upon the
long line of devoted patriots, who, throughout history,
have truly loved their country; and, upon all, who,
in noble aspirations for the general good and in for-
getfulness of self, have stood out before their age,
and gathered into their generous bosoms the shafts of
tyranny and wrong, in order to make a pathway for
Truth. You discredit Luther, when alone he nailed
his articles to the door of the church at Wittenberg,
and then, to the imperial demand that he should re-
tract, firmly replied, "Here I stand; I cannot do
otherwise, so help me God!" You discredit Hamp-
den, when alone he refused to pay the few shillings of
ship-money, and shook the throne of Charles I.; you
discredit Milton, when, amidst the corruptions of a
heartless Court, he lived on, the lofty friend of

Liberty, above question of suspicion; you discredit Russell and Sidney, when, for the sake of their country, they calmly turned from family and friends, to tread the narrow steps of the scaffold; you discredit those early founders of American institutions, who preferred the hardships of a wilderness, surrounded by a savage foe, to injustice on beds of ease; you discredit our later fathers, who, few in numbers and weak in resources, yet strong in their cause, did not hesitate to brave the 'mighty power of England, already encircling the globe with her morning drumbeats. Yes, sir, of such are the fanatics of history, according to the Senator. But I tell that Senator, that there are characters badly eminent, of whose fanaticism there can be no question. Such were the ancient Egyptians, who worshipped divinities in brutish forms; the Druids, who darkened the forests of oak, in which they lived, by sacrifices of blood; the Mexicans, who surrendered countless victims to the propitiation of their obscene idols; the Spaniards, who, under Alva, sought to force the Inquisition upon Holland, by a tyranny kindred to that now employed to force Slavery upon Kansas; and such were the Algerines, when in solemn conclave, after listening to a speech not unlike that of the Senator from South Carolina, they resolved to continue the slavery of white Christians, and to extend it to the countrymen of Washington! Aye, sir, extend it! And in this same dreary catalogue faithful history must record all who now, in an enlightened age and in a land of boasted Freedom, stand up, in perversion of the Constitution and in denial of immortal truth, to fasten a new shackle upon their fellow-man. If the Senator wishes to see fanatics, let him look round among his own associates; let him look at himself.

But I have not done with the Senator. There is

another matter regarded by him of such consequence,
that he interpolated it into the speech of the Senator
from New Hampshire [Mr. HALE], and also announced
that he had prepared himself with it, to take in his
pocket all the way to Boston, when he expected to
address the people of that community. On this account, and for the sake of truth, I stop for one
moment, and tread it to the earth. The North, according to the Senator, was engaged in the slave
trade, and helped to introduce slaves into the Southern
States ; and this undeniable fact he proposed to establish by statistics, in stating which his errors surpassed
his sentences in number. But I let these pass for the
present, that I may deal with his argument. Pray,
sir, is the acknowledged turpitude of a departed generation to become an example for us? And yet the
suggestion of the Senator, if entitled to any consideration in this discussion, must have this extent. I
join my friend from New Hampshire in thanking the
Senator from South Carolina for adducing this instance ; for it gives me an opportunity to say, that
the Northern merchants, with homes in Boston,
Bristol, Newport, New York, and Philadelphia, who
catered for Slavery during the years of the slave
trade, are the lineal progenitors of the Northern men,
with homes in these places, who lend themselves to
Slavery in our day ; and especially that all, whether
North or South, who take part, directly or indirectly,
in the conspiracy against Kansas, do but continue the
work of the slave traders, which you condemn. It is
true, too true, alas ! that our fathers were engaged in
this traffic ; but that is no apology for it. And in
repelling the authority of this example, I repel also
the trite argument founded on the earlier example of
England. It is true that our mother country, at the
peace of Utrecht, extorted from Spain the Assiento

Contract, securing the monopoly of the slave trade with the Spanish Colonies, as the whole price of all the blood of great victories; that she higgled at Aix-la-Chapelle for another lease of this exclusive traffic; and again, at the treaty of Madrid, clung to the wretched piracy. It is true, that in this spirit the power of the mother country was prostituted to the same base ends in her American Colonies, against indignant protests from our fathers. All these things now rise up in judgment against her. Let us not follow the Senator from South Carolina to do the very evil to-day, which in another generation we condemn.

As the Senator from South Carolina is the Don Quixote, the Senator from Illinois [Mr. DOUGLAS] is the squire of Slavery, its very Sancho Panza, ready to do all its humiliating offices. This Senator, in his laboured address, vindicating his laboured report — piling one mass of elaborate error upon another mass — constrained himself, as you will remember, to unfamiliar decencies of speech. Of that address I have nothing to say at this moment, though before I sit down I shall show something of its fallacies. But I go back now to an earlier occasion, when true to his native impulses, he threw into this discussion, " for a charm of powerful trouble," personalities most discreditable to this body. I will not stop to repel the imputations which he cast upon myself; but I mention them to remind you of the " sweltered venom sleeping got," which, with other poisoned ingredients, he cast into the cauldron of this debate. Of other things I speak. Standing on this floor, the Senator issued his rescript, requiring submission to the Usurped Power of Kansas; and this was accompanied by a manner — all his own — such as befits the tyrannical threat. Very well. Let the Senator try.

G

I tell him now that he cannot enforce any such submission. The Senator, with the Slave Power at his back, is strong; but he is not strong enough for this purpose. He is bold. He shrinks from nothing. Like Danton, he may cry, "*l'audace! l'audace! toujours l'audace!*" but even his audacity cannot compass this work. The Senator copies the British officer, who, with boastful swagger, said that with the hilt of his sword he would cram the "stamps" down the throats of the American people, and he will meet a similar failure. He may convulse this country with civil feud. Like the ancient madman, he may set fire to this Temple of Constitutional Liberty, grander than Ephesian dome; but he cannot enforce obedience to that tyrannical usurpation.

The Senator dreams that he can subdue the North. He disclaims the open threat, but his conduct still implies it. How little that Senator knows himself, or the strength of the cause which he persecutes! He is but a mortal man; against him is an immortal principle. With finite power he wrestles with the infinite, and he must fall. Against him are stronger battalions than any marshalled by mortal arm—the inborn, ineradicable, invincible sentiments of the human heart; against him is nature in all her subtle forces; against him is God. Let him try to subdue these.

But I pass from these things, which, though belonging to the very heart of the discussion, are yet preliminary in character, and press at once to the main question.

I. It belongs to me now, in the first place, to expose the CRIME AGAINST KANSAS, in its origin and extent. Logically, this is the beginning of the argument. I say Crime, and deliberately adopt this strongest term, as better than any other denoting the consummate transgression. I would go further, if language could further go. It is the *Crime of Crimes* — surpassing far the old *crimen majestatis*, pursued with vengeance by the laws of Rome, and containing all other crimes, as the greater contains the less. I do not go too far, when I call it the *Crime against Nature*, from which the soul recoils, and which language refuses to describe. To lay bare this enormity, I now proceed. The whole subject has already become a twice-told tale, and its renewed recital will be a renewal of its sorrow and shame; but I shall not hesitate to enter upon it. The occasion requires it from the beginning.

It has been well remarked by a distinguished historian of our country, that, at the Ithuriel touch of the Missouri discussion, the slave interest, hitherto hardly recognised as a distinct element in our system, started up portentous and dilated, with threats and assumptions, which are the origin of our existing national politics. This was in 1820. The discussion ended with the admission of Missouri as a slaveholding State, and the prohibition of Slavery in all the remaining territory west of the Mississippi, and north of 36° 30′, leaving the condition of other territory south of this line, or subsequently acquired, untouched by the arrangement. Here was a solemn act of legislation, called at the time a compromise, a covenant, a compact, first brought forward in this body by a slaveholder—vindicated by slaveholders in debate—finally sanctioned by slaveholding votes—also upheld at the time by the essential approbation of a slaveholding President, James Monroe and his Cabinet, of whom a majority were slaveholders, including Mr. Calhoun himself; and this compromise was made the condition of the admission of Missouri, without which that State could not have been received into the Union. The bargain was simple, and was applicable, of course, only to the territory named. Leaving all other territory to await the judgment of another generation, the South said to the North, Conquer your prejudices so far as to admit Missouri as a Slave State, and, in consideration of this much-coveted boon, Slavery shall be prohibited for ever in all the remaining Louisiana Territory above 36° 30'; and the North yielded.

In total disregard of history, the President, in his annual message, has told us that this compromise "was *reluctantly* acquiesced in by the Southern States." Just the contrary is true. It was the work of slaveholders, and was crowded by their concurring votes upon a reluctant North. At the time it was hailed by slaveholders as a victory. Charles Pinckney, of South Carolina, in an oft-quoted letter, written at three o'clock on the night of its passage, says, "It is considered here by the slaveholding States as a great triumph." At the North it was accepted as a defeat, and the friends of freedom everywhere throughout the country bowed their heads with mortification. But little did they know the completeness of their disaster. Little did they dream that the prohibition of Slavery in the Territory, which was stipulated as the price of their fatal capitulation, would also at the very moment of its maturity be wrested from them.

Time passed, and it became necessary to provide for this Territory an organised Government. Suddenly, without notice in the public press, or the prayer of a single petition, or one word of open recommendation from the President — after an acquiescence of thirty-three years, and the irreclaimable possession by the South of its special share under this compromise — in violation of every obligation of honour, compact, and good neighbourhood—and in contemptuous disregard of the out-gushing sentiments of an aroused North, this time-honoured prohibition, in itself a landmark of freedom, was overturned, and the vast region now known as Kansas and Nebraska was opened to Slavery. It was natural that a measure thus repugnant in character should be pressed by arguments mutually repugnant. It was urged on two principal reasons, so opposite and inconsistent as to slap each other in the face—one being that, by the repeal of the prohibition, the Territory would be left open to the entry of slaveholders with their slaves, without hindrance; and the other being, that the people would be left absolutely free to determine the question for themselves, and to prohibit the entry of slaveholders with their slaves, if they should think best. With some, the apology was the alleged rights of slaveholders; with others, it was the alleged rights of the people. With some, it was openly the extension of Slavery; and with others, it was openly the establishment of Freedom, under the guise of popular sovereignty. Of course, the measure, thus upheld in defiance of reason, was carried through Congress in defiance of all the securities of legislation; and I mention these things that you may see in what foulness the present Crime was engendered.

It was carried, *first*, by *whipping in* to its support, through executive influence and patronage, men who acted against their own declared judgment and the known will of their constituents. *Secondly*, by *foisting out of place*, both in the Senate and House of Representatives, important business, long pending, and usurping its room. *Thirdly*, by *trampling under foot* the rules of the House of Representatives, always before the safeguard of the minority. And *fourthly*, by *driving it to a close* during the very session in which it originated, so that it might not be arrested by the indignant voice of the people. Such are some of the means by which this snap judgment was obtained. If the clear will of the people had not been disregarded, it could not have passed. If the Government had not nefariously interposed its influence, it could not have passed. If it had been left to its natural place in the order of business, it could not have passed. If the rules of the House and the rights of the minority had not been violated, it could not have passed. If it had been allowed to go over to another Congress, when the people might be heard, it would have been ended; and then the crime we now deplore, would have been without its first seminal life.

Mr. President, I mean to keep absolutely within the limits of parliamentary propriety. I make no personal imputations; but only with frankness, such as belongs to the occasion and my own character, describe a great historical act, which is now enrolled in the Capitol. Sir, the Nebraska Bill was in every respect a swindle. It was a swindle by the South of the North. It was, on the part of those who had already completely enjoyed their share of the Missouri compromise, a swindle of those whose share was yet absolutely untouched; and the plea of unconstitutionality set up — like the plea of usury after the borrowed money has been enjoyed — did not make it less a swindle. Urged as a Bill of Peace, it was a swindle of the whole country. Urged as opening the doors to slave-masters with their slaves, it was a swindle of the asserted doctrine of popular sovereignty. Urged as sanctioning popular sovereignty,

It was a swindle of the asserted rights of slave-masters. It was a swindle of a broad territory, thus cheated of protection against Slavery. It was a swindle of a great cause, early espoused by Washington, Franklin, and Jefferson, surrounded by the best fathers of the Republic. Sir, it was a swindle of God-given inalienable rights. Turn it over; look at it on all sides, and it is everywhere a swindle; and, if the word I now employ has not the authority of classical usage, it has, on this occasion, the indubitable authority of fitness. No other word will adequately express the mingled meanness and wickedness of the cheat.

Its character was still further apparent in the general structure of the Bill. Amidst overflowing professions of regard for the sovereignty of the people in the Territory, they were despoiled of every essential privilege of sovereignty. They were not allowed to choose their Governor, Secretary, Chief Justice, Associate Justices, Attorney, or Marshal — all of whom are sent from Washington; nor were they allowed to regulate the salaries of any of these functionaries, or the daily allowance of the legislative body, or even the pay of the clerks and doorkeepers; but they were left free to adopt Slavery. And this was called popular sovereignty! Time does not allow, nor does the occasion require, that I should stop to dwell on this transparent device to cover a transcendent wrong. Suffice it to say, that Slavery is in itself an arrogant denial of human rights, and by no human reason can the power to establish such a wrong be placed among the attributes of any just sovereignty. In refusing it such a place, I do not deny popular rights, but uphold them; I do not restrain popular rights, but extend them. And, sir, to this conclusion you must yet come, unless deaf, not only to the admonitions of political justice, but also to the genius of our own Constitution, under which, when properly interpreted, no valid claim for Slavery can be set up anywhere in the national territory. The Senator from Michigan [Mr. CASS] may say, in response to the Senator from Mississippi [Mr. BROWN], that Slavery cannot go into the Territory under the Constitution, without legislative introduction; and permit me to add, in response to both, that Slavery cannot go there at all. *Nothing can come out of nothing;* and there is absolutely nothing in the Constitution out of which Slavery can be derived, while there are provisions, which, when properly interpreted, make its existence anywhere within the exclusive national jurisdiction impossible.

The offensive provision in the Bill was in its form a legislative anomaly, utterly wanting the natural directness and simplicity of an honest transaction. It did not undertake openly to repeal the old prohibition of Slavery, but seemed to mince the matter, as if conscious of the swindle. It said that this prohibition, "being inconsistent with the principle of non-intervention by Congress with Slavery in the States and Territories, as recognised by the legislation of 1850, commonly called the Compromise Measures, is hereby declared inoperative and void." Thus, with insidious ostentation, was it pretended that an act, violating the greatest compromise of our legislative history, and setting loose the foundations of all compromise, was derived out of a compromise. Then followed in the Bill the further declaration, which is entirely without precedent, and which has been aptly called " a stump speech in its belly," namely: "it being the true intent and meaning of this act, not to legislate Slavery into any Territory or State, nor to exclude it therefrom, but to leave the

people thereof perfectly free to form and regulate
their domestic institutions in their own way, subject
only to the Constitution of the United States." Here
were smooth words, such as belong to a cunning
tongue enlisted in a bad cause. But whatever may
have been their various hidden meanings, this at
least was evident, that by their effect, the Congressional Prohibition of Slavery, which had always been
regarded as a seven-fold shield, covering the whole
Louisiana Territory north of 36° 30', was now removed, while a principle was declared, which would
render the supplementary prohibition of Slavery in
Minnesota, Oregon, and Washington, " inoperative
and void," and thus open to Slavery all these vast
regions, now the rude cradles of mighty States.
Here you see the magnitude of the mischief con-
templated. But my purpose now is with the Crime
against Kansas, and I shall not stop to expose the
conspiracy beyond.

Mr. President, men are wisely presumed to intend
the natural consequences of their conduct, and to
seek what their acts seem to promote. Now, the
Nebraska Bill, on its very face, openly cleared the
way for Slavery, and it is not wrong to presume that
its originators intended the natural consequences of
such an act, and sought in this way to extend
Slavery. Of course, they did. And this is the first
stage in the Crime against Kansas.

But this was speedily followed by other develop-
ments. The bare-faced scheme was soon whispered,
that Kansas must be a Slave State. In conformity
with this idea was the Government of this unhappy
Territory organised in all its departments ; and thus
did the President, by whose complicity the Prohibition of Slavery had been overthrown, lend himself to
a new complicity — giving to the conspirators a lease

of connivance, amounting even to copartnership.
The Governor, Secretary, Chief Justice, Associate
Justices, Attorney, and Marshal, with a whole caucus
of other stipendiaries, nominated by the President
and confirmed by the Senate, were all commended as
friendly to Slavery. No man, with the sentiments
of Washington, or Jefferson, or Franklin, found any
favour; nor is it too much to say, that, had these
great patriots once more come among us, not one of
them, with his recorded unretracted opinions on
Slavery, could have been nominated by the President
or confirmed by the Senate for any post in that
Territory. With such auspices the conspiracy proceeded. Even in advance of the Nebraska Bill,
secret societies were organised in Missouri, ostensibly
to protect her institutions, and afterwards, under the
name of " Self-Defensive Associations," and of " Blue
Lodges," these were multiplied throughout the western counties of that State, *before any counter-movement from the North.* It was confidently anticipated,
that by the activity of these societies, and the interest
of slaveholders everywhere, with the advantage derived from the neighbourhood of Missouri, and the
influence of the Territorial Government, Slavery
might be introduced into Kansas, quietly but surely,
without arousing a conflict — that the crocodile egg
might be stealthily dropped in the sun-burnt soil,
there to be hatched unobserved until it sent forth its
reptile monster.

But the conspiracy was unexpectedly balked. The
debate, which convulsed Congress, had stirred the
whole country. Attention from all sides was directed upon Kansas, which at once became the favourite goal of emigration. The Bill had loudly
declared, that its object was " to leave the people
perfectly free to form and regulate their domestic

institutions in their own way;" and its supporters everywhere challenged the determination of the question between Freedom and Slavery by a competition of emigration. Thus, while opening the Territory to Slavery, the Bill also opened it to emigrants from every quarter, who might by their votes redress the wrong. The populous North, stung by a sharp sense of outrage, and inspired by a noble cause, poured into the debatable land, and promised soon to establish a supremacy of numbers there, involving, of course, a just supremacy of Freedom.

Then was conceived the consummation of the Crime against Kansas. What could not be accomplished peaceably, was to be accomplished forcibly. The reptile monster, that could not be quietly and securely hatched there, was to be pushed full-grown into the Territory. All efforts were now given to the dismal work of forcing Slavery on Free Soil. In flagrant derogation of the very Popular Sovereignty, whose name helped to impose this Bill upon the country, the atrocious object was now distinctly avowed. And the avowal has been followed by the act. Slavery has been forcibly introduced into Kansas, and placed under the formal safeguards of pretended law. How this was done, belongs to the argument.

In depicting this consummation, the simplest outline, without one word of colour, will be best. Whether regarded in its mass or its details, in its origin or its result, it is all blackness, illumined by nothing from itself, but only by the heroism of the undaunted men and women whom it environed. A plain statement of facts will be a picture of fearful truth, which faithful history will preserve in its darkest gallery. In the foreground all will recognise a familiar character, in himself a connecting link between the President and the border ruffian — less conspicuous for ability

than for the exalted place he has occupied — who once
sat in the seat where you now sit, sir; where once sat
John Adams and Thomas Jefferson; also, where once
sat Aaron Burr.   I need not add the name of David
R. Atchison.   You have not forgotten that, at the
session of Congress immediately succeeding the Nebraska Bill, he came tardily to his duty here, and
then, after a short time, disappeared.   The secret has
been long since disclosed.   Like Catiline, he stalked
into this Chamber, reeking with conspiracy — *immo
in Senatum venit* — and then like Catiline he skulked
away — *abiit, excessit, evasit, erupit* — to join and provoke the conspirators, who at a distance awaited their
congenial chief.   Under the influence of his malign
presence the Crime ripened to its fatal fruits, while
the similitude with Catiline was again renewed in the
sympathy, not even concealed, which he found in the
very Senate itself, where, beyond even the Roman
example, a Senator has not hesitated to appear as his
open compurgator.

And now, as I proceed to show the way in which
this Territory was overrun and finally subjugated to
Slavery, I desire to remove in advance all question
with regard to the authority on which I rely.   The
evidence is secondary; but it is the best which, in the
nature of the case, can be had, and it is not less clear,
direct, and peremptory, than any by which we are
assured of the campaigns in the Crimea or the fall of
Sevastopol.   In its manifold mass, I confidently assert,
that it is such a body of evidence as the human mind
is not able to resist.   It is found in the concurring
reports of the public press; in the letters of corre-
spondents; in the testimony of travellers; and in the
unaffected story to which I have listened from leading
citizens, who, during this winter, have "come flock-
ing" here from that distant Territory.   It breaks

forth in the irrepressible outcry, reaching us from Kansas, in truthful tones, which leave no ground of mistake. It addresses us in formal complaints, instinct with the indignation of a people determined to be free, and unimpeachable as the declarations of a murdered man on his dying bed against his murderer. And let me add, that all this testimony finds an echo in the very statute-book of the conspirators, and also in language dropped from the President of the United States.

I begin with an admission from the President himself, in whose sight the people of Kansas have little favour. And yet, after arraigning the innocent emigrants from the North, he was constrained to declare that their conduct was " far from justifying the *illegal* and *reprehensible* counter-movement which ensued." Then, by the reluctant admission of the Chief Magistrate, there was a counter-movement, at once *illegal* and *reprehensible*. I thank thee, President, for teaching me these words ; and I now put them in the front of this exposition, as in themselves a confession. Sir, this " illegal and reprehensible counter-movement " is none other than the dreadful Crime — under an apologetic *alias* — by which, through successive invasions, Slavery has been forcibly planted in this Territory.

Next to this Presidential admission must be placed the details of the invasions, which I now present as not only "illegal and reprehensible," but also unquestionable evidence of the resulting Crime.

The violence, for some time threatened, broke forth on the 29th November, 1854, at the first election of a Delegate to Congress, when companies from Missouri, amounting to upwards of one thousand, crossed into Kansas, and, with force and arms, proceeded to vote for Mr. Whitfield, the candidate of Slavery. An eye-witness, General Pomeroy, of superior intelligence and perfect integrity, thus describes this scene:—

" The first ballot-box that was opened upon our virgin soil was closed to us by overpowering numbers and impending force. So bold and reckless were our invaders, that they cared not to conceal their attack. They came upon us not in the guise of voters, to steal away our franchise, but boldly and openly to snatch it with a strong hand. They came directly from their own homes, and in compact and organised bands, with arms in hand and provisions for the expedition, marched to our polls, and, when their work was done, returned whence they came."

Here was an outrage at which the coolest blood of patriotism boils. Though, for various reasons unnecessary to develop, the busy settlers allowed the election to pass uncontested, still the means employed were none the less "illegal and reprehensible."

This infliction was a significant prelude to the grand invasion of the 30th March, 1855, at the election of the first Territorial Legislature under the organic law, when an armed multitude from Missouri entered the Territory, in larger numbers than General Taylor commanded at Buena Vista, or than General Jackson had within his lines at New Orleans—larger far than our fathers rallied on Bunker Hill. On they came as an "army with banners," organised in companies, with officers, munitions, tents, and provisions, as though marching upon a foreign foe, and breathing loud-mouthed threats that they would carry their purpose, if need be, by the bowie-knife and revolver. Among them, according to his own confession, was David R. Atchison, belted with the vulgar arms of his vulgar comrades. Arrived at their several destinations on the night before the election, the invaders pitched their tents, placed their sentries, and waited for the coming day. The same trustworthy eye-witness, whom I have already quoted, says, of one locality : —

"Baggage-waggons were there, with arms and ammunition enough for a protracted fight, and among them two brass field-pieces, ready charged. They came with drums beating and flags flying, and their leaders were of the most prominent and conspicuous men of their State."

Of another locality he says : —

"The invaders came together in one armed and organised body, with trains of fifty waggons, besides horsemen, and, the night before election, pitched their camp in the vicinity of the polls ; and, having appointed their own judges in place of those who, from intimidation or otherwise, failed to attend, they voted without any proof of residence."

With this force they were able, on the succeeding day, in some places, to intimidate the judges of elections; in others, to substitute judges of their own appointment; in others, to wrest the ballot-boxes from their rightful possessors, and everywhere to exercise a complete control of the election, and thus, by a preternatural audacity of usurpation, impose a Legislature upon the free people of Kansas. Thus was conquered the Sevastopol of that Territory!

But it was not enough to secure the Legislature. The election of a member of Congress recurred on the 2nd October, 1855, and the same foreigners, who had learned their strength, again manifested it. Another invasion, in controlling numbers, came from Missouri, and once more forcibly exercised the electoral franchise in Kansas.

At last, in the latter days of November, 1855, a storm, long brewing, burst upon the heads of the devoted people. The ballot-boxes had been violated,

and a Legislature installed, which had proceeded to
carry out the conspiracy of the invaders ; but the
good people of the Territory, born to Freedom, and
educated as American citizens, showed no signs of
submission. Slavery, though recognised by pretended
law, was in many places practically an outlaw.   To
the lawless borderers, this was hard to bear ; and,
like the Heathen of old, they raged, particularly
against the town of Lawrence, already known, by
the firmness of its principles and the character of its
citizens, as the citadel of the good cause.   On this
account they threatened, in their peculiar language,
to " wipe it out."   Soon the hostile power was
gathered for this purpose.   The wickedness of this
invasion was enhanced by the way in which it began.

A citizen of Kansas, by the name of Dow, was murdered by one of the partisans of Slavery, under the
name of "law and order."   Such an outrage naturally
aroused indignation and provoked threats.   The pro-
fessors of " law and order " allowed the murderer to
escape ; and, still further to illustrate the irony of
the name they assumed, seized the friend of the murdered man, whose few neighbours soon rallied for his
rescue.   This transaction, though totally disregarded
in its chief front of wickedness, became the excuse for
unprecedented excitement.   The weak Governor, with
no faculty higher than servility to Slavery — whom
the President, in his official delinquency, had appointed to a trust worthy only of a well-balanced
character — was frightened from his propriety.   By
proclamation he invoked the Territory.   By telegraph
he invoked the President.   The Territory would not
respond to his senseless appeal.   The President was
dumb ; but the proclamation was circulated throughout the border counties of Missouri ; and Platte, Clay,
Carlisle, Sabine, Howard, and Jefferson, each of them,

contributed a volunteer company, recruited from the road sides, and armed with weapons which chance afforded — known as the " shot-gun militia " — with a Missouri officer as commissary general, dispensing rations, and another Missouri officer as general-in-chief; with two waggon loads of rifles, belonging to Missouri, drawn by six mules, from its arsenal at Jefferson City ; with seven pieces of cannon, belonging to the United States, from its arsenal at Liberty; and this formidable force, amounting to at least 1800 men, terrible with threats, with oaths, and with whisky, crossed the borders, and encamped in larger part at Wacherusa, over against the doomed town of Lawrence, which was now threatened with destruction. With these invaders was the Governor, who by this act levied war upon the people he was sent to protect. In camp with him was the original Catiline of the conspiracy, while by his side was the docile Chief Justice and the docile Judges. But this is not the first instance in which an unjust Governor has found tools where he ought to have found justice. In the great impeachment of Warren Hastings, the British orator, by whom it was conducted, exclaims, in words strictly applicable to the misdeed I now arraign, " Had he not the Chief Justice, the tamed and domesticated Chief Justice who waited on him like a familiar spirit ? " Thus was this invasion countenanced by those who should have stood in the breach against it. For more than a week it continued, while deadly conflict seemed imminent. I do not dwell on the heroism by which it was encountered, or the mean retreat to which it was compelled; for that is not necessary to exhibit the Crime which you are to judge. But I cannot forbear to add other additional features, furnished in the letter of a clergy-

H

man, written at the time, who saw and was a part of what he describes:—

"Our citizens have been shot at, *and in two instances murdered,* our houses invaded, hay-ricks burnt, corn and other provisions plundered, cattle driven off, all communication cut off between us and the States, waggons on the way to us with provisions stopped and plundered, and the drivers taken prisoners, and we in hourly expectation of an attack. *Nearly every man has been in arms in the village.* Fortifications have been thrown up, by incessant labour night and day. The sound of the drum and the tramp of armed men resounded through our streets, *families fleeing with their household goods for safety.* Day before yesterday, the report of cannon was heard at our house from the direction of Lecompton. Last Thursday one of our neighbours — one of the most peaceable and excellent of men, from Ohio — on his way home, was set upon by a gang of twelve men on horseback, and shot down. Over eight hundred men are gathered under arms at Lawrence. As yet, no act of violence has been perpetrated by those on our side. *No blood of retaliation stains our hands. We stand and are ready to act purely in the defence of our homes and lives.*"

But the catalogue is not yet complete. On the 15th of December, when the people assembled to vote on the Constitution then submitted for adoption — only a few days after the Treaty of Peace between the Governor on the one side and the town of Lawrence on the other—another and fifth irruption was made. But I leave all this untold. Enough of these details has been given. Five several times and more have these invaders entered Kansas in armed array, and thus five several times and more have they trampled upon the organic law of the Territory. But these extraordinary expeditions are simply the extraordinary witnesses to successive uninterrupted violence. They stand out conspicuous, but not alone. The spirit of evil, in which they had their origin, was

wakeful and incessant. From the beginning, it hung
upon the skirts of this interesting Territory, harrow-
ing its peace, disturbing its prosperity, and keeping
its inhabitants under the painful alarms of war. Thus
was all security of person, of property, and of labour,
overthrown; and when I urge this incontrovertible
fact, I set forth a wrong which is small only by the
side of the giant wrong, for the consummation of
which all this was done.

Sir, what is man—what is government—without security; in the absence of which, nor man nor government can proceed in development or enjoy the fruits of
existence? Without security, civilisation is cramped
and dwarfed. Without security, there can be no true
Freedom. Nor shall I say too much, when I declare
that security, guarded of course by its offspring, Freedom, is the true end and aim of government. Of this
indispensable boon the people of Kansas have thus far
been despoiled—absolutely, totally. All this is aggravated by the nature of their pursuits, rendering them
peculiarly sensitive to interruption, and at the same
time attesting their innocence. They are for the most
part engaged in the cultivation of the soil, which from
time immemorial has been the sweet employment of
undisturbed industry. Contented in the returns of
bounteous nature and the shade of his own trees, the
husbandman is not aggressive; accustomed to produce, and not to destroy, he is essentially peaceful,
unless his home is invaded, when his arm derives
vigour from the soil he treads, and his soul inspiration from the heavens beneath whose canopy he daily
toils. And such are the people of Kansas, whose
security has been overthrown. Scenes from which
civilisation averts her countenance have been a part
of their daily life. The border incursions, which, in
barbarous ages or barbarous lands, have fretted and

"harried" an exposed people, have been here renewed, with this peculiarity, that our border robbers do not simply levy black mail and drive off a few cattle, like those who acted under the inspiration of the Douglas of other days; that they do not seize a few persons, and sweep them away into captivity, like the African slave-traders whom we brand as pirates; but that they commit a succession of acts, in which all border sorrows and all African wrongs are revived together on American soil, and which for the time being annuls all protection of all kinds, and enslaves the whole Territory.

Private griefs mingle their poignancy with public wrongs. I do not dwell on the anxieties which families have undergone, exposed to sudden assault, and obliged to lie down to rest with the alarms of war ringing in their ears, not knowing that another day might be spared to them. Throughout this bitter winter, with the thermometer at 30° below zero, the citizens of Lawrence have been constrained to sleep under arms, with sentinels treading their constant watch against surprise. But our souls are wrung by individual instances. In vain do we condemn the cruelties of another age, the refinements of torture to which men have been doomed—the rack and thumb-screw of the Inquisition, the last agonies of the regicide Ravaillac—"Luke's iron crown, and Damien's bed of steel"—for kindred outrages have disgraced these borders. Murder has stalked, assassination has skulked in the tall grass of the prairie, and the vindictiveness of man has assumed unwonted forms. A preacher of the Gospel of the Saviour has been ridden on a rail, and then thrown into the Missouri, fastened to a log, and left to drift down its muddy, tortuous current. And lately we have had the tidings of that enormity without precedent — a deed without a name — where a candidate for the Legislature was most brutally gashed with knives and hatchets, and then, after weltering in blood on the snow-clad earth, was trundled along with gaping wounds, to fall dead in the face of his wife. It is common to drop a tear of sympathy over the trembling solicitudes of our early fathers, exposed to the stealthy assault of the savage foe; and an eminent American artist has pictured this scene in a marble group of rare beauty, on the front of the National Capitol, where the uplifted tomahawk is arrested by the strong arm and generous countenance of the pioneer, while his wife and children find shelter at his feet; but now the tear must be dropped over the trembling solicitudes of fellow-citizens, seeking to build a new State in Kansas, and exposed to the perpetual assault of murderous robbers from Missouri. Hirelings, picked from the drunken spew and vomit of an uneasy civilisation, in the form of men —

> " Aye, in the catalogue ye go for men:
> As hounds and gray-hounds, mongrels, spaniels, curs,
> Shoughs, water-rugs, and demi-wolves, are called
> All by the name of dogs,"—

leashed together by secret signs and lodges, have renewed the incredible atrocities of the Assassins and of the Thugs; showing the blind submission of the Assassins to the Old Man of the Mountain, in robbing Christians on the road to Jerusalem, and showing the heartlessness of the Thugs, who, avowing that murder was their religion, waylaid travellers on the great road from Agra to Delhi; with the more deadly bowie-knife for the dagger of the Assassin, and the more deadly revolver for the noose of the Thug.

In these invasions, attended by the entire subversion of all security in this Territory, with the plun-

der of the ballot-box, and the pollution of the electoral
franchise, I show simply the process in unprecedented
crime.   If that be the best Government, where an
injury to a single citizen is resented as an injury to
the whole State, then must our Government forfeit
all claim to any such eminence, while it leaves its
citizens thus exposed.   In the outrage upon the ballot-box, even without the illicit fruits which I shall
soon exhibit, there is a peculiar crime of the deepest
dye, though subordinate to the final Crime, which
should be promptly avenged.   In countries where
royalty is upheld, it is a special offence to rob the
crown jewels, which are the emblems of that sovereignty before which the loyal subject bows, and it
is treason to be found in adultery with the Queen,
for in this way may a false heir be imposed upon the
State; but in our Republic the ballot-box is the single
priceless jewel of that sovereignty which we respect,
and the electoral franchise, out of which are born the
rulers of a free people, is the Queen whom we are to
guard against pollution.   In this plain presentment,
whether as regards Security, or as regards Elections,
there is enough, surely, without proceeding further,
to justify the intervention of Congress, most promptly
and completely, to throw over this oppressed people
the impenetrable shield of the Constitution and laws.
But the half is not yet told.

As every point in a wide-spread horizon radiates
from a common centre, so everything said or done in
this vast circle of Crime radiates from the *One Idea*,
that Kansas, at all hazards, must be made a Slave
State.   In all the manifold wickednesses that have
occurred, and in every successive invasion, this *One
Idea* has been ever present, as the Satanic tempter—
the motive power—the *causing cause*.

To accomplish this result, three things were at-

tempted : *first*, by outrages of all kinds to drive the
friends of Freedom, already there, out of the Territory; *secondly*, to deter others from coming; and
thirdly, to obtain the complete control of the Government. The process of driving out, and also of de-
terring, has failed. On the contrary, the friends of
Freedom there became more fixed in their resolves
to stay and fight the battle, which they had never
sought, but from which they disdained to retreat;
while the friends of Freedom elsewhere were more
aroused to the duty of timely succours, by men and
munitions of just self-defence.

But, while defeated in the first two processes proposed, the conspirators succeeded in the last. By the
violence already portrayed at the election of the 30th
March, when the polls were occupied by the armed
hordes from Missouri, they imposed a Legislature
upon the Territory, and thus, under the iron mask of
law, established a Usurpation not less complete than
any in history. That this was done, I proceed to
prove. Here is the evidence:

1. Only in this way can this extraordinary expedition be adequately explained. In the words of Mo-
lière, once employed by John Quincy Adams in the
other House, *Que diable allaient-ils faire dans cette
galère?* What did they go into the Territory for?
If their purposes were peaceful, as has been suggested, why cannons, arms, flags, numbers, and all
this violence? As simple citizens, proceeding to the
honest exercise of the electoral franchise, they might
have gone with nothing more than a pilgrim's staff.
Philosophy always seeks a *sufficient cause*, and only in
the *One Idea*, already presented, can a cause be found
in any degreee commensurate with this Crime; and
this becomes so only when we consider the mad fanaticism of Slavery.

H 4

2. Public notoriety steps forward to confirm the suggestion of reason. In every place where Truth can freely travel, it has been asserted and understood, that the Legislature was imposed upon Kansas by foreigners from Missouri ; and this universal voice is now received as undeniable verity.

3. It is also attested by the harangues of the conspirators. Here is what Stringfellow said *before* the invasion :

" To those who have qualms of conscience as to violating laws, State or National, the time has come when such impositions must be disregarded, as your rights and property are in danger; *and I advise you, one and all, to enter every election district in Kansas, in defiance of Reeder and his vile myrmidons, and vote at the point of the bowie-knife and revolver.* Neither give nor take quarter, as our case demands it. It is enough that the slave-holding interest wills it, from which there is no appeal. What right has Governor Reeder to rule Missourians in Kansas ? His proclamation and prescribed oath must be repudiated. It is your interest to do so. Mind that Slavery is established where it is not prohibited."

Here is what Atchison said *after* the invasion :

"Well, what next? Why an election for members of the Legislature to organise the Territory must be held. What did I advise you to do then? Why, meet them on their own ground, and beat them at their own game again; and cold and inclement as the weather was, I went over with a company of men. My object in going was not to vote. I had no right to vote, unless I had disfranchised myself in Missouri. I was not within two miles of a voting place. My object in going was not to vote, but to settle a difficulty between two of our candidates ; and the Abolitionists of the North said, *and published it abroad, that Atchison was there with bowie-knife and revolver, and by God 'twas true. I never did go into that Territory—I never intend to go into that Territory—without being prepared for all such kind of cattle.* Well, we beat them, and Governor Reeder gave certificates to a majority of all the members of both Houses, and then, after they were organised, as everybody will admit, they were the only competent persons to say who were, and who were not, members of the same."

4. It is confirmed by the contemporaneous admission of the *Squatter Sovereign*, a paper published at Atchison, and at once the organ of the President and of these borderers, which, under date of 1st April, thus recounts the victory :

" INDEPENDENCE, [MISSOURI,] *March* 31. 1855.

" Several hundred emigrants from Kansas have just entered our city. They were preceded by the Westport and Independence brass bands. They came in at the west side of the public square, and proceeded entirely around it, the bands cheering us with fine music, and the emigrants with good news. Immediately following the bands were about two hundred horsemen in regular order; following these were one hundred and fifty waggons, carriages, &c. They gave repeated cheers for Kansas and Missouri. They report that not an Anti-Slavery man will be in the Legislature of Kansas. *We have made a clean sweep.*"

5. It is also confirmed by the contemporaneous testimony of another paper, always faithful to Slavery, the New York *Herald,* in the letter of a correspondent from Brunswick, in Missouri, under date of 20th April, 1855 :

" From five to seven thousand men started from Missouri to attend the election, some to remove, but the most to return to their families, with an intention, if they liked the Territory, to make it their permanent abode at the earliest moment practicable. But they intended to vote. The Missourians were, many of them, Douglas men. There were one hundred and fifty voters from this county, one hundred and seventy-five from Howard, one hundred from Cooper. Indeed, every county furnished its quota; and when they set out, it looked

like an army." . . . . . . "They were armed." . . . . . .
"And, as there were no houses in the Territory, they carried tents.   Their mission was a peaceable one—to vote, and
to drive down stakes for their future homes. After the election,
some one thousand five hundred of the voters sent a committee to Mr. Reeder, to ascertain if it was his purpose to
ratify the election.   He answered that it was, and said the
majority at an election must carry the day.   But it is not to
be denied that the one thousand five hundred, apprehending
that the Governor might attempt to play the tyrant—since
his conduct had already been insidious and unjust—wore on
their hats bunches of hemp.   They were resolved, if a tyrant
attempted to trample upon the rights of the sovereign people,
to hang him."

6. It is again confirmed by the testimony of a
lady, who for five years has lived in Western Missouri, and thus writes in a letter published in the
New Haven Register:

"MIAMI, SALINE CO., *November* 26. 1855.

" You ask me to tell you something about the Kansas and
Missouri troubles.   Of course you know in what they have
originated.   *There is no denying that the Missourians have
determined to control the elections, if possible;* and I don't know
that their measures would be justifiable, except upon the principle of self-preservation ; and that, you know, is the first law
of nature."

7. And it is confirmed still further by the Circular
of the Emigration Society of Lafayette, in Missouri,
dated as late as 25th March, 1856, in which the
efforts of Missourians are openly confessed:

" The Western counties of Missouri have for the last two
years been heavily taxed, both in money and time, in fighting
the battles of the South.   *Lafayette county alone has expended
more than $100,000 in money, and as much or more in time.
Up to this time, the border counties of Missouri have upheld
and maintained the rights and interests of the South in this*

struggle, unassisted, and not unsuccessfully. But the Abolitionists, staking their all upon the Kansas issue, and hesitating at no means, fair or foul, are moving heaven and earth to render that beautiful Territory a *Free State.*"

8. Here, also, is complete admission of the Usurpation, by the *Intelligencer*, a leading paper of St. Louis, Missouri, made in the ensuing summer:

" Atchison and Stringfellow, with their Missouri followers, overwhelmed the settlers in Kansas, browbeat and bullied them, and took the Government from their hands. Missouri votes elected the present body of men who insult public intelligence and popular rights by styling themselves ' The Legislature of Kansas.' This body of men are helping themselves to fat speculations by locating the 'seat of Government' and getting town lots for their votes. They are passing laws disfranchising all the citizens of Kansas who do not believe Negro Slavery to be a Christian institution and a national blessing. They are proposing to punish with imprisonment the utterance of views inconsistent with their own. And they are trying to perpetuate their preposterous and infernal tyranny by appointing *for a term of years* creatures of their own, as commissioners in every county, to lay and collect taxes, and see that the laws they are passing are faithfully executed. Has this age anything to compare with these acts in audacity ?"

9. In harmony with all these is the authoritative declaration of Governor Reeder, in a speech addressed to his neighbours, at Easton, Pennsylvania, at the end of April, 1855, and immediately afterwards published in the Washington *Union*. Here it is:

"It was indeed too true that Kansas had been invaded, conquered, subjugated, by an armed force from beyond her borders, led on by a fanatical spirit, trampling under foot the principles of the Kansas bill and the right of suffrage."

10. And in similar harmony is the complaint of the

people of Kansas, in a public meeting at Big Springs, on the 5th September, 1855, embodied in these words:

"*Resolved,* That the body of men who for the last two months have been passing laws for the people of our Territory, moved, counselled, and dictated to by the demagogues of Missouri, are to us a foreign body representing only the lawless invaders who elected them, and not the people in the Territory—that we repudiate their action as the monstrous consummation of an act of violence, usurpation, and fraud, unparalleled in the history of the Union, and worthy only of men unfitted for the duties and regardless of the responsibilities of Republicans."

11. And finally, by the official minutes, which have been laid on our table by the President, the invasion which ended in the Usurpation, is clearly established; but the effect of this testimony has been so amply exposed by the Senator from Vermont [Mr. COLLAMER], in his able and indefatigable argument, that I content myself with simply referring to it.

On this cumulative, irresistible evidence, in concurrence with the antecedent history, I rest. And yet senators here have argued that this cannot be so —precisely as the conspiracy of Catiline was doubted in the Roman Senate. *Nonnulli sunt in hoc ordine, qui aut ea, quæ imminent, non videant; aut ea, quæ vident, dissimulent; qui spem Catilinæ mollibus sententiis aluerunt, conjurationemque nascentem non credendo corroboraverunt.* As I listened to the Senator from Illinois, while he painfully strove to show that there was no Usurpation, I was reminded of the effort by a distinguished logician, in a much-admired argument, to prove that Napoleon Bonaparte never existed. And permit me to say, that the fact of his existence is not placed more completely above doubt than the fact of this Usurpation. This I assert on the proofs already presented. But confirmation comes almost while I speak. The columns of the public press are now daily filled with testimony, solemnly taken before the Committee of Congress in Kansas, which shows, in awful light, the violence ending in the Usurpation. Of this I may speak on some other occasion. Meanwhile I proceed with the development of the Crime.

The usurping Legislature assembled at the appointed place in the interior, and then at once, in opposition to the veto of the Governor, by a majority of two-thirds, removed to the Shawnee Mission, a place in most convenient proximity to the Missouri borderers, by whom it had been constituted, and whose tyrannical agent it was. The statutes of Missouri, in all their text, with their divisions and subdivisions, were adopted bodily, and with such little local adaptation that the word " State " in the original is not even changed to " Territory," but is left to be corrected by an explanatory act. But, all this general legislation was entirely subordinate to the special act, entitled " An Act to punish Offences against Slave Property," in which the One Idea, that provoked this whole conspiracy, is at last embodied in legislative form, and Human Slavery openly recognised on Free Soil, under the sanction of pretended law. This act of thirteen sections is in itself a *Dance of Death*. But its complex completeness of wickedness, without a parallel, may be partially conceived, when it is understood that in three sections only of it is the penalty of death denounced no less than forty-eight different times, by as many changes of language, against the heinous offence, described in forty-eight different ways, of interfering with what does not exist in that Territory — and under the Constitution cannot exist there — I mean property in human flesh. Thus is Liberty sacrificed to Slavery, and Death summoned to sit at the gates as guardian of the Wrong.

But the work of Usurpation was not perfected even yet. It had already cost too much to be left at any hazard.

> "To be thus was nothing;
> But to be safely thus!"

Such was the object. And this could not be, except by the entire prostration of all the safeguards of Human Rights. The liberty of speech, which is the very breath of a Republic; the press, which is the terror of wrong-doers; the bar, through which the oppressed beards the arrogance of law; the jury, by which right is vindicated; all these must be struck down, while officers are provided, in all places, ready to be the tools of this tyranny; and then, to obtain final assurance that their crime was secure, the whole Usurpation, stretching over the Territory, must be fastened and riveted by legislative bolts, spikes, and screws, *so as to defy all effort at change through the ordinary forms of law.* To this work, in its various parts, were bent the subtlest energies; and never, from Tubal Cain to this hour, was any fabric forged with more desperate skill and completeness.

Mark, sir, three different legislative enactments, which constitute part of this work. *First*, according to one act, all who deny, by spoken or written word, " the right of persons to hold Slaves in this Territory," are denounced as felons, to be punished by imprison· ment at hard labour, for a term not less than two years; it may be for life. And to show the extravagance of this injustice, it has been well put by the Senator from Vermont [Mr. COLLAMER], that should the Senator from Michigan [Mr. CASS], who believes

that Slavery cannot exist in a Territory, unless introduced by express legislative acts, venture there
with his moderate opinions, his doom must be that
of a felon!   To this extent are the great liberties of
speech and of the press subverted. *Secondly*, by
another act, entitled " An Act concerning Attorneys-
at-Law," no person can practice as an attorney, unless
he *shall obtain a license* from the Territorial courts,
which, of course, a tyrannical discretion will be free
to deny; and, after obtaining such license, he is constrained to take an oath, not only " to support " the
Constitution of the United States, but also to " support and sustain "—mark here the reduplication—
the Territorial Act, and the Fugitive Slave Bill, thus
erecting a test for the function of the bar, calculated
to exclude citizens who honestly regard that latter
legislative enormity as unfit to be obeyed. And,
thirdly, by another act, entitled " An Act concerning
Jurors," all persons, " conscientiously opposed to holding slaves," or " not admitting the right to hold slaves
in the Territory," are excluded from the jury on every
question, civil or criminal, arising out of asserted
slave property; while, in all cases, the summoning
of the jury is left without one word of restraint to
" the marshal, sheriff, or other officer," who are thus
free to pack it according to their tyrannical discretion.

For the ready enforcement of all statutes against
human freedom, the President had already furnished
a powerful quota of officers, in the Governor, Chief
Justice, Judges, Secretary, Attorney, and Marshal.
The Legislature completed this part of the work by
constituting, in each county, a *Board of Commissioners*, composed of two persons, associated with the
Probate Judge, whose duty it is " to appoint a county
treasurer, coroner, justices of the peace, constables,

and *all* other officers provided for by law," and then proceeded to the choice of this very Board ; thus delegating and diffusing their usurped power, and tyrannically imposing upon the Territory a crowd of officers, in whose appointment the people have had no voice, directly or indirectly.

And still the final inexorable work remained. A Legislature renovated in both branches, could not assemble until 1858, so that, during this long intermediate period, this whole system must continue in the likeness of law, unless overturned by the Federal Government, or, in default of such interposition, by a generous uprising of an oppressed people. But it was necessary to guard against the possibility of change, even tardily, at a future election; and this was done by two different acts ; under the *first* of which, all who will not take the oath to support the Fugitive Slave Bill are excluded from the elective franchise; and under the *second* of which, all others are entitled to vote who shall tender a tax of one dollar to the Sheriff on the day of election; thus by provision of Territorial law, disfranchising all opposed to Slavery, and at the same time opening the door to the votes of the invaders; by an unconstitutional shibboleth, excluding from the polls the mass of actual settlers, and by making the franchise depend upon a petty tax only, admitting to the polls the mass of borderers from Missouri. Thus, by tyrannical forethought, the Usurpation not only fortified all that it did, but assumed a *self-perpetuating* energy.

Thus was the Crime consummated. Slavery now stands erect, clanking its chains on the Territory of Kansas, surrounded by a code of death, and trampling upon all cherished liberties, whether of speech, the press, the bar, the trial by jury, or the electoral franchise. And, sir, all this has been done, not merely to introduce a wrong which in itself is a denial of all rights, and in dread of which a mother has lately taken the life of her offspring; not merely, as has been sometimes said, to protect Slavery in Missouri, since it is futile for this State to complain of freedom on the side of Kansas, when freedom exists without complaint on the side of Iowa, and also on the side of Illinois; but it has been done for the sake of political power, in order to bring two new slave-holding Senators upon this floor, and thus to fortify in the National Government the desperate chances of a waning Oligarchy. As the ship, voyaging on pleasant summer seas, is assailed by a pirate crew, and robbed for the sake of its doubloons and dollars — so is this beautiful Territory now assailed in its peace and prosperity, and robbed, in order to wrest its political power to the side of Slavery. Even now the black flag of the land pirates from Missouri waves at the mast head; in their laws you hear the pirate yell, and see the flash of the pirate knife; while, incredible to relate! the President, gathering the Slave Power at his back, testifies a pirate sympathy.

Sir, all this was done in the name of popular sovereignty. And this is the close of the tragedy. Popular sovereignty, which, when truly understood, is a fountain of just power, has ended in popular slavery; not merely in the subjection of the unhappy African race, but of this proud Caucasian blood, which you boast. The profession with which you began, of *All by the People*, has been lost in the wretched reality of *Nothing for the People*. Popular sovereignty, in whose deceitful name plighted faith was broken, and an ancient landmark of freedom was overturned, now lifts itself before us, like Sin, in the terrible picture of Milton,—

I

" That seemed a woman to the waist, and fair,
But ended foul in many a scaly fold
Voluminous and vast, a serpent armed
With mortal sting; about her middle round
A cry of hell-hounds never ceasing barked
With wide Cerberean mouths full loud, and rung
A hideous peal; yet when they list, would creep,
If aught disturbed their noise, into her womb,
And kennel there, yet there still barked and howled
Within, unseen."

The image is complete at all points; and with this exposure, I take my leave of the Crime against Kansas.

II. Emerging from all the blackness of this Crime, in which we seem to have been lost, as in a savage wood, and turning our backs upon it, as upon desolation and death, from which, while others have suffered, we have escaped, I come now to THE APOLOGIES which the Crime has found. Sir, well may you start at the suggestion that such a series of wrongs, so clearly proved by various testimony, so openly confessed by the wrong-doers, and so widely recognised throughout the country, should find Apologies. But the partisan spirit, now, as in other days, hesitates at nothing. The great crimes of history have never been without Apologies. The massacre of St. Bartholomew, which you now instinctively condemn, was, at the time, applauded in high quarters, and even commemorated by a papal medal, which may still be procured at Rome; as the Crime against Kansas, which is hardly less conspicuous in dreadful eminence, has been shielded on this floor by extenuating words, and even by a Presidential message, which, like the Papal medal, can never be forgotten in considering the madness and perversity of men.

Sir, the Crime cannot be denied. The President himself has admitted "illegal and reprehensible" conduct. To such conclusion he was compelled by irresistible evidence: but what he mildly describes I openly arraign. Senators may affect to put it aside by a sneer; or to reason it away by figures; or to explain it by a theory, such as desperate invention has produced on this floor, that the assassins and Thugs of Missouri were in reality citizens of Kansas; but all these efforts, so far as made, are only tokens of the weakness of the cause, while to the original Crime they add another offence of false testimony against innocent and suffering men. But the Apologies for the Crime are worse than the efforts at denial. In cruelty and heartlessness they identify their authors with the great transgression.

They are four in number, and fourfold in character. The first is the Apology *tyrannical;* the second, the Apology *imbecile;* the third, the Apology *absurd;* and the fourth, the Apology *infamous.* This is all. Tyranny, imbecility, absurdity, and infamy, all unite to dance, like the weird sisters, about this Crime.

The Apology *tyrannical* is founded on the mistaken act of Governor Reeder, in authenticating the usurping Legislature, by which it is asserted that, whatever may have been the actual force or fraud in its election, the people of Kansas are effectually concluded, and the whole proceeding is placed under the formal sanction of law. According to this assumption, complaint is now in vain, and it only remains that Congress should sit and hearken to it, without correcting the wrong, as the ancient tyrant listened and granted no redress to the human moans that issued from the heated brazen bull which subtle cruelty had

devised.   This I call the Apology of technicality inspired by tyranny.

The facts on this head are few and plain. Governor
Reeder, after allowing only five days for objections
to the returns—a space of time unreasonably brief in
that extensive territory — declared a majority of the
members of the Council and of the House of Representatives " duly elected," withheld certificates from
certain others, because of satisfactory proof that
they were not duly elected, and appointed a day for
new elections to supply these vacancies. Afterwards,
by formal message, he recognised the Legislature as
a legal body, and when he vetoed their act of adjournment to the neighbourhood of Missouri, he did it
simply on the ground of the illegality of such an
adjournment under the organic law.   Now, to every
assumption founded on these facts, there are two
satisfactory replies ; *first*, that no certificate of the
Governor can do more than authenticate a subsisting
legal act, without of itself infusing legality where the
essence of legality is not already ; and *secondly*, that
violence or fraud, wherever disclosed, vitiates completely every proceeding.   In denying these principles, you place the certificate above the thing
certified, and give a perpetual lease to violence and
fraud, merely because at an ephemeral moment they
were unquestioned.   This will not do.

Sir, I am no apologist for Governor Reeder.   There
is sad reason to believe that he went to Kansas ori-
ginally as the tool of the President ; but his simple
nature, nurtured in the atmosphere of Pennsylvania,
revolted at the service required, and he turned from
his patron to duty.   Grievously did he err in yielding
to the Legislature any act of authentication ; but he
has in some measure answered for this error by de-

termined efforts since to expose the utter illegality of that body, which he now repudiates entirely. It was said of certain Roman Emperors, who did infinite mischief in their beginnings, and infinite good towards their ends, that they should never have been born, or never died; and I would apply the same to the official life of this Kansas Governor. At all events, I dismiss the Apology founded on his acts, as the utterance of tyranny by the voice of law, transcending the declaration of the pedantic judge, in the British Parliament, on the eve of our Revolution, that our fathers, notwithstanding their complaints, were in reality represented in Parliament, inasmuch as their lands, under the original charters, were held "in common socage, as of the manor of Greenwich in Kent," which, being duly represented, carried with it all the Colonies. Thus in other ages has tyranny assumed the voice of law.

Next comes the Apology *imbecile*, which is founded on the alleged want of power in the President to arrest this Crime. It is openly asserted, that, under the existing laws of the United States, the Chief Magistrate had no authority to interfere in Kansas for this purpose. Such is the broad statement, which, even if correct, furnishes no apology for any proposed ratification of the Crime, but which is in reality untrue; and this, I call the Apology of imbecility.

In other matters, no such ostentatious imbecility appears. Only lately, a vessel of war in the Pacific has chastised the cannibals of the Fejee Islands, for alleged outrages on American citizens. But no person of ordinary intelligence will pretend that American citizens in the Pacific have received wrongs from these cannibals comparable in atrocity to those received by American citizens in Kansas. Ah, sir,

the interests of Slavery are not touched by any chastisement of the Fejees!

Constantly we are informed of efforts at New York,
through the agency of the Government, and sometimes only on the breath of suspicion, to arrest vessels about to sail on foreign voyages in violation of
our neutrality laws or treaty stipulation. Now, no
man familiar with the cases will presume to suggest
that the urgency for these arrests was equal to the
urgency for interposition against these successive
invasions from Missouri. But the Slave Power is
not disturbed by such arrests at New York!

At this moment, the President exults in the vigilance with which he has prevented the enlistment of
a few soldiers, to be carried off to Halifax, in violation of our territorial sovereignty, and England is
bravely threatened, even to the extent of a rupture
of diplomatic relations, for her endeavour, though
unsuccessful, and at once abandoned. Surely, no
man in his senses will urge that this act was anything but trivial by the side of the Crime against
Kansas. But the Slave Power is not concerned in
this controversy.

Thus, where the Slave Power is indifferent, the
President will see that the laws are faithfully executed; but, in other cases, where the interests of
Slavery are at stake, he is controlled absolutely by
this tyranny, ready at all times to do, or not to do,
precisely as it dictates. Therefore it is, that Kansas
is left a prey to the Propagandists of Slavery, while
the whole Treasury, the Army and Navy of the
United States, are lavished to hunt a single slave
through the streets of Boston. You have not forgotten the latter instance; but I choose to refresh it
in your minds.

As long ago as 1851, the War Department and

Navy Department concurred in placing the forces of the United States, near Boston, at the command of the Marshal, if needed, for the enforcement of an Act of Congress, which had no support in the public conscience, as I believe it has no support in the Constitution; and thus these forces were degraded to the loathsome work of slave-hunters. More than three years afterwards, an occasion arose for their intervention. A fugitive from Virginia, who for some days had trod the streets of Boston as a freeman, was seized as a slave. The whole community was aroused, while Bunker Hill and Faneuil Hall quaked with responsive indignation. Then, sir, the President, anxious that no tittle of Slavery should suffer, was curiously eager in the enforcement of the statute. The despatches between him and his agents in Boston attest his zeal. Here are some of them: —

"BOSTON, *May* 27. 1854.

" *To the President of the United States*:

"In consequence of an attack upon the Court-house, last night, for the purpose of rescuing a fugitive slave, under arrest, and in which one of my own guards was killed, *I have availed myself of the resources of the United States, placed under my control by letter from the War and Navy Departments, in* 1851, and now have two companies of troops, from Fort Independence, stationed in the Court-house. Everything is now quiet. The attack was repulsed by my own guard.

"WATSON FREEMAN,
" *United States Marshal, Boston, Mass.*"

"WASHINGTON, *May* 27. 1854.

" *To Watson Freeman,*
" *United States Marshal, Boston, Mass.*

"Your conduct is approved. The law must be executed.
"FRANKLIN PIERCE."

I 4

"WASHINGTON, *May* 30. 1854.

" *To Hon. B. F. Hallet, Boston, Mass.* :

" What is the state of the case of Burns ?

"SIDNEY WEBSTER,

" [*Private Secretary of the President.*]"

"WASHINGTON, *May* 31. 1854.

"* To B. F. Hallett,*

" *United States Attorney, Boston, Mass.* :

" Incur any expense deemed necessary by the Marshal and yourself, for City Military, or otherwise, to insure the execution of the law.

"FRANKLIN PIERCE."

But the President was not content with such forces as were then on hand in the neighbourhood. Other posts also were put under requisition. Two companies of National troops, stationed at New York, were kept under arms, ready at any moment to proceed to Boston; and the Adjutant General of the Army was directed to repair to the scene, there to superintend the execution of the statute. All this was done for the sake of Slavery; but during long months of menace suspended over the Free Soil of Kansas, breaking forth in successive invasions, the President has folded his hands in complete listlessness, or, if he has moved at all, it has been only to encourage the robber propagandists.

And now the intelligence of the country is insulted by the Apology, that the President had no power to interfere. Why, sir, to make this confession is to confess our Government to be a practical failure — which I will never do, except, indeed, as it is administered now. No, sir; the imbecility of the Chief Magistrate shall not be charged upon our American Institutions. Where there is a will, there is a way; and in his case, had the will existed, there would have been a way, easy and triumphant, to guard against the Crime we now deplore. His powers were in every respect ample; and this I will prove by the statute book. By the Act of Congress of 28th February, 1795, it is enacted, " that whenever the laws of the United States shall be opposed, *or the execution thereof obstructed*, in any State, by combinations too powerful to be suppressed by the ordinary course of judicial proceedings, or by the powers vested in the marshals," the President " may call forth the militia." By the supplementary Act of 3rd March, 1807, in all cases where he is authorised to call forth the militia " for the purpose of causing the laws to be duly executed," the President is further empowered, in any State *or Territory*, " to employ for the same purposes such part of the land or naval force of the United States as shall be judged necessary." There is the letter of the law; and you will please to mark the power conferred. In no case where the *laws of the United States* are *opposed*, or their execution *obstructed*, is the President constrained to wait for the requisition of a Governor, or even the petition of a citizen. Just so soon as he learns the fact, no matter by what channel, he is invested by law with full power to counteract it. True it is, that when the *laws of a State* are obstructed, he can interfere only on the application of the Legislature of such State, or of the Executive, when the Legislature cannot be convened; but when the Federal laws are obstructed, no such preliminary application is necessary. It is his high duty, under his oath of office, to see that they are executed, and, if need be, by the Federal forces.

And, sir, this is the precise exigency that has arisen in Kansas — precisely this; nor more, nor less. The Act of Congress, constituting the very *organic law* of the Territory, which, in peculiar phrase, as if to avoid ambiguity, declares, as " its true intent and meaning," that the people thereof " shall be left perfectly free to form and regulate their domestic institutions in their own way," has been from the beginning *opposed* and *obstructed* in its execution. If the President had power to employ the Federal forces in Boston, when he supposed the Fugitive Slave Bill was obstructed, and merely in anticipation of such obstruction, it is absurd to say that he had not power in Kansas, when, in the face of the whole country, the very *organic law* of the Territory was trampled under foot by succes- sive invasions, and the freedom of the people there overthrown. To assert ignorance of this obstruc- tion — premeditated, long-continued, and stretching through months — attributes to him not merely im- becility, but idiocy. And thus do I dispose of this Apology.

Next comes the Apology *absurd*, which is, indeed, in the nature of a pretext. It is alleged that a small printed pamphlet, containing the " Constitution and Ritual of the Grand Encampment and Regiments of the Kansas Legion," was taken from the person of one George F. Warren, who attempted to avoid de- tection by chewing it. The oaths and grandiose titles of the pretended Legion have all been set forth, and this poor mummery of a secret society, which existed only on paper, has been gravely introduced on this floor, in order to extenuate the Crime against Kansas. It has been paraded in more than one speech, and even stuffed into the report of the com- mittee.

A part of the obligations assumed by the members of this Legion shows why it has been thus pursued, and also attests its innocence. It is as follows :

" I will never knowingly propose a person for membership in this order *who is not in favour of making Kansas a free State,* and whom I feel satisfied will exert his entire influence to bring about this result. I will support, maintain, and abide by any honourable movement made by the organisation to secure this great end, *which will not conflict with the laws of the country and the Constitution of the United States.*"

Kansas is to be made a free State, by an honourable movement, which will not conflict with the laws and the Constitution. That is the object of the organisation, declared in the very words of the initiatory obligation. Where is the wrong in this? What is there here, which can cast reproach, or even suspicion, upon the people of Kansas? Grant that the Legion was constituted, can you extract from it any Apology for the original Crime, or for its present ratification? Secret societies, with their extravagant oaths, are justly offensive; but who can find, in this mistaken machinery, any excuse for the denial of all rights to the people of Kansas? All this, I say, on the supposition that the society was a reality, which it was not. Existing in the fantastic brains of a few persons only, it never had any practical life. It was never organised. The whole tale, with the mode of obtaining the copy of the Constitution, is at once a cock-and-bull story and a mare's nest; trivial as the former; absurd as the latter; and to be dismissed, with the Apology founded upon it, to the derision which triviality and absurdity justly receive.

It only remains, under this head, that I should speak of the Apology *infamous;* founded on false testimony against the Emigrant Aid Company, and assumptions of duty more false than the testimony. Defying truth and mocking decency, this Apology excels all others in futility and audacity, while, from its utter hollowness, it proves the utter impotence of the conspirators to defend their Crime.   Falsehood, always *infamous*, in this case arouses peculiar scorn. An association of sincere benevolence, faithful to the Constitution and laws, whose only fortifications are hotels, school-houses, and churches; whose only weapons are saw-mills, tools, and books; whose mission is peace and good will, has been falsely assailed on this floor, and an errand of blameless virtue has been made the pretext for an unpardonable Crime. Nay, more—the innocent are sacrificed, and the guilty set at liberty.   They who seek to do the mission of the Saviour are scourged and crucified, while the murderer, Barabbas, with the sympathy of the chief priests, goes at large.

Were I to take counsel of my own feelings, I should dismiss this whole Apology to the ineffable contempt which it deserves ; but it has been made to play such a part in this conspiracy, that I feel it a duty to expose it completely.*

III. From this ample survey, where one obstruction after another has been removed, I now pass, in the third place, to the consideration of the *various remedies proposed*, ending with the TRUE REMEDY.

The Remedy should be co-extensive with the original Wrong; and since, by the passage of the Nebraska Bill, not only Kansas, but also Nebraska, Minnesota, Washington, and even Oregon, have been opened to Slavery, the original Prohibition should be restored to its complete activity throughout these various Territories.   By such a happy restoration, made in good faith, the whole country would be replaced in the condition which it enjoyed before the

---

* *Some passages in defence of the Emigrant Aid Society, uninteresting to an European reader, are omitted.*—ED.

introduction of that dishonest measure. Here is the Alpha and the Omega of our aim in this immediate controversy. But no such extensive measure is now in question. The Crime against Kansas has been special, and all else is absorbed in the special remedies for it. Of these I shall now speak.

As the Apologies were fourfold, so are the Remedies proposed fourfold, and they range themselves in natural order, under designations which so truly disclose their character as even to supersede argument. First, we have the Remedy of Tyranny; next, the Remedy of Folly; next, the Remedy of Injustice and Civil War; and fourthly, the Remedy of Justice and Peace. There are the four caskets; and you are to determine which shall be opened by Senatorial votes.

There is the *Remedy of Tyranny*, which, like its complement, the Apology of Tyranny — though espoused on this floor, especially by the Senator from Illinois — proceeds from the President, and is embodied in a special message. It proposes to enforce obedience to the existing laws of Kansas, " whether Federal or *local*," when, in fact, Kansas has no "local" laws except those imposed by the Usurpation from Missouri, and it calls for additional appropriations to complete this work of tyranny.

I shall not follow the President in his elaborate endeavour to prejudge the contested election now pending in the House of Representatives; for this whole matter belongs to the privileges of that body, and neither the President nor the Senate has a right to intermeddle therewith. I do not touch it. But now, while dismissing it, I should not pardon myself, if I failed to add, that any person who founds his claim to a seat in Congress on the pretended votes of

* 17

hirelings from another State, with no home on the
soil of Kansas, plays the part of Anacharsis Clootz,
who, at the bar of the French Convention, undertook
to represent nations that knew him not, or, if they
knew him, scorned him; with this difference, that in
our American case, the excessive farce of the transaction cannot cover its tragedy.   But all this I put
aside — to deal only with what is legitimately before
the Senate.

I expose simply the Tyranny which upholds the
existing Usurpation, and asks for additional appropriations.   Let it be judged by an example, from which
in this country there can be no appeal.   Here is the
speech of George III., made from the Throne to Parliament, in response to the complaints of the Province
of Massachusetts Bay, which, though smarting under
laws passed by usurped power, had yet avoided all
armed opposition, while Lexington and Bunker Hill
still slumbered in rural solitude, unconscious of the
historic kindred which they were soon to claim.   Instead of Massachusetts Bay, in the Royal speech,
substitute Kansas, and the message of the President
will be found fresh on the lips of the British King.
Listen now to the words, which, in opening Parliament, 30th November, 1774, his Majesty, according
to the official report, was pleased to speak : —

" *My Lords and Gentlemen :*

" It gives me much concern that I am obliged, at the
opening of this Parliament, to inform you that a most daring
spirit of resistance and disobedience to the law still unhappily
prevails in the Province of the *Massachusetts Bay*, and has
in divers parts of it broke forth in fresh violences of a very
criminal nature.   *These proceedings have been countenanced
in other of my Colonies,* and *unwarrantable attempts have been
made to obstruct the Commerce of this Kingdom, by unlawful
combinations.*   I have taken such measures and given such

orders as I have judged most proper and effectual *for carrying into execution the laws which were passed in the last session of the late Parliament*, for the protection and security of the Commerce of my subjects, and for the restoring and preserving peace, order, and good government, in the Province of the *Massachusetts Bay*."—*American Archives*, 4th series, vol. i. page 1465.

The King complained of a " daring spirit of resistance and disobedience to the law ;" so also does the President. The King adds, that it has " broke forth in fresh violences of a very criminal nature ;" so also does the President. The King declares that these proceedings have been "countenanced and encouraged in other of my Colonies;" even so the President declares that Kansas has found sympathy in " remote States." The King inveighs against " unwarrantable measures " and " unlawful combinations ;" even so inveighs the President. The King proclaims that he has taken the necessary steps " for carrying into execution the laws," passed in defiance of the constitutional rights of the Colonies ; even so the President proclaims that he shall " exert the whole power of the Federal Executive " to support the Usurpation in Kansas. The parallel is complete. The Message, if not copied from the Speech of the King, has been fashioned on the same original block, and must be dismissed to the same limbo. I dismiss its tyrannical assumptions in favour of the Usurpation. I dismiss also its petition for additional appropriations in the affected desire to maintain order in Kansas. It is not money or troops that you need there ; but simply the good will of the President. That is all, absolutely. Let his complicity with the Crime cease, and peace will be restored. For myself, I will not consent to wad the National artillery with fresh appropriation bills, when its murderous hail is to be directed against the constitutional rights of my fellow-citizens.

Next comes the *Remedy of Folly*, which, indeed, is also a Remedy of Tyranny; but its Folly is so surpassing as to eclipse even its Tyranny. It does not proceed from the President. With this proposition he is not in any way chargeable. It comes from the Senator from South Carolina, who, at the close of a long speech, offered it as his single contribution to the adjustment of this question, and who thus far stands alone in its support. It might, therefore, fitly bear his name; but that which I now give to it is a more suggestive synonym.

This proposition, nakedly expressed, is that the people of Kansas should be deprived of their arms. That I may not do the least injustice to the Senator, I quote his precise words:

" The President of the United States is under the highest and most solemn obligations to interpose; and if I were to indicate the manner in which he should interpose in Kansas, I would point out the old common law process. I would serve a warrant on Sharpe's rifles, and if Sharpe's rifles did not answer the summons, and come into court on a day certain, or if they resisted the sheriff, I would summon the *posse comitatus*, and would have Colonel Sumner's regiment to be a part of that *posse comitatus*."

Really, sir, has it come to this? The rifle has ever been the companion of the pioneer, and, under God, his tutelary protector against the red man and the beast of the forest. Never was this efficient weapon more needed in just self-defence, than now in Kansas, and at least one article in our National Constitution must be blotted out, before the complete right to it can in any way be impeached. And yet such is the madness of the hour, that, in defiance of the solemn

guaranty, embodied in the Amendments to the Constitution, that "the right of the people to keep and
bear arms shall not be infringed," the people of
Kansas have been arraigned for keeping and bearing
them, and the Senator from South Carolina has had
the face to say openly, on this floor, that they should
be disarmed—of course, that the fanatics of Slavery,
his allies and constituents, may meet no impediment.
Sir, the Senator is venerable with years; he is reputed
also to have worn at home, in the State which he
represents, judicial honours; and he is placed here at
the head of an important Committee occupied particularly with questions of law; but neither his years,
nor his position, past or present, can give respecta-
bility to the demand he has made, or save him from
indignant condemnation, when, to compass the
wretched purposes of a wretched cause, he thus proposes to trample on one of the plainest provisions of
constitutional liberty.

Next comes the *Remedy of Injustice and Civil War*
—organised by Act of Congress. This proposition,
which is also an offshoot of the original Remedy of
Tyranny, proceeds from the Senator from Illinois
[Mr. DOUGLAS], with the sanction of the Committee
on Territories, and is embodied in the Bill which is
now pressed to a vote.

By this Bill it is proposed, as follows:—

"That whenever it shall appear, by a census to be taken
under the direction of the Governor, by the authority of the
Legislature, that there shall be 93,420 inhabitants (that being
the number required by the present ratio of representation
for a member of Congress) within the limits hereafter described as the Territory of Kansas, *the Legislature of said
Territory shall be, and is hereby, authorised to provide by law
for the election of delegates,* by the people of said Territory, to assemble in Convention and form a Constitution and

* K

State Government, preparatory to their admission into the Union on an equal footing with the original States in all respects whatsoever, by the name of the State of Kansas."

Now, sir, consider these words carefully, and you will see that, however plausible and velvet-pawed they may seem, yet in reality they are most unjust and cruel. While affecting to initiate honest proceedings for the formation of a State, they furnish to this Territory no redress for the Crime under which it suffers; nay, they recognise the very Usurpation, in which the Crime ended, and proceed to endow it with new prerogatives. It is *by the authority of the Legislature* that the census is to be taken, which is the first step in the work. It is also *by the authority of the Legislature* that a Convention is to be called for the formation of a Constitution, which is the second step. But the Legislature is not obliged to take either of these steps. To its absolute wilfulness is it left to act or not to act in the premises. And since, in the ordinary course of business, there can be no action of the Legislature till January of the next year, all these steps, which are preliminary in their character, are postponed till after that distant day— thus keeping this great question open, to distract and irritate the country. Clearly this is not what is required. The country desires peace at once, and is determined to have it. But this objection is slight by the side of the glaring Tyranny, that, in recognising the Legislature, and conferring upon it these new powers, the Bill recognises the existing Usurpation, not only as the authentic Government of the Territory for the time being, but also as possessing a creative power to reproduce itself in the new State. Pass this Bill, and you enlist Congress in the conspiracy, not only to keep the people of Kansas in their present subjugation, throughout their territorial existence, but also to protract this subjugation into their existence as a State, while you legalise and perpetuate the very *force* by which Slavery has been already planted there.

I know that there is another deceptive clause, which seems to throw certain safeguards around the election of delegates to the Convention, *when the Convention shall be ordered by the Legislature;* but out of this very clause do I draw a condemnation of the Usurpation which the Bill recognises. It provides that the tests, coupled with the electoral franchise, shall not prevail in the election of delegates, and thus impliedly condemns them. But if they are not to prevail on this occasion, why are they permitted at the election of the Legislature? If they are unjust in the one case, they are unjust in the other. If annulled at the election of delegates, they should be annulled at the election of the Legislature; *whereas the Bill of the Senator leaves all these offensive tests in full activity at the election of the very Legislature out of which this whole proceeding is to come,* and it leaves the polls at both elections in the control of the officers appointed by the Usurpation. Consider well the facts. By an existing statute, establishing the Fugitive Slave Bill as a shibboleth, a large portion of the honest citizens are excluded from voting for the Legislature, while, by another statute, all who present themselves with a fee of one dollar, whether from Missouri or not, and who can utter this shibboleth, are entitled to vote. And it is a Legislature thus chosen, under the auspices of officers appointed by the Usurpation, that you now propose to invest with parental powers to rear the Territory into a State. You recognise and confirm the Usurpation, which you ought to annul without delay. You put the infant State, now preparing to take a place in our sisterhood, to suckle

with the wolf, which you ought at once to kill. The
improbable story of Baron Münchausen is verified.
The bear, which thrust itself into the harness of the
horse it had devoured, and then whirled the sledge
according to mere brutal bent, is recognised by this
bill, and kept in its usurped place, when the safety of
all requires that it should be shot.

In characterising this Bill as the Remedy of Injustice and Civil War, I give it a plain, self-evident
title. It is a continuation of the Crime against
Kansas, and as such deserves the same condemnation.
It can only be defended by those who defend the
Crime. Sir, you cannot expect that the people of
Kansas will submit to the Usurpation which this bill
sets up, and bids them bow before — as the Austrian
tyrant set up his cap in the Swiss market-place. If
you madly persevere, Kansas will not be without her
William Tell, who will refuse at all hazards to recognise the tyrannical edict; and this will be the beginning of civil war.

Next, and lastly, comes the *Remedy of Justice and
Peace,* proposed by the Senator from New York,
[Mr. SEWARD,] and embodied in his Bill for the immediate admission of Kansas as a State of this Union,
now pending as a substitute for the bill of the
Senator from Illinois. This is sustained by the
prayer of the people of the Territory, setting forth
a Constitution formed by a spontaneous movement;
in which all there had opportunity to participate,
without distinction of party. Rarely has any proposition, so simple in character, so entirely practicable, so absolutely within your power, been presented, which promised at once such beneficent
results. In its adoption, the Crime against Kansas
will be all happily absolved, the Usurpation which it

established will be peacefully suppressed, and order will be permanently secured. By a joyful metamorphosis, this fair Territory may be saved from outrage.

> " Oh help," she cries, " in this extremest need,
> If you who hear are Deities indeed;
> Gape earth, and make for this dread foe a tomb,
> *Or change my form, whence all my sorrows come.*"

In offering this proposition, the Senator from New York has entitled himself to the gratitude of the country. He has, throughout a life of unsurpassed industry, and of eminent ability, done much for Freedom, which the world will not let die; but he has done nothing more opportune than this, and he has uttered no words more effective than the speech, so masterly and ingenious, by which he has vindicated it.*

Mr. President, an immense space has been traversed, and I now stand at the goal. The argument in its various parts is here closed. The Crime against Kansas has been displayed in its origin and extent, beginning with the overthrow of the Prohibition of Slavery; next cropping out in conspiracy on the borders of Missouri; then hardening into a continuity of outrage, through organised invasions and miscellaneous assaults, in which all security was destroyed, and ending at last in the perfect subjugation of a generous people to an unprecedented Usurpation. Turning aghast from the Crime, which, like murder, seemed to confess itself " with most miraculous organ," we have looked with mingled shame and indignation upon the four Apologies, whether of

* *Some passages are omitted in which technical objections to the admission of Kansas are answered.*—ED.

K 3

Tyranny, Imbecility, Absurdity, or Infamy, in which it has been wrapped, marking especially the false testimony, congenial with the original crime, against the Emigrant Aid Company. Then were noted, in succession, the four Remedies, whether of Tyranny— Folly — Injustice and Civil War — or Justice and Peace, which last bids Kansas, in conformity with past precedents, and under the exigencies of the hour, in order to redeem her from Usurpation, to take a place as a sovereign State of the Union; and this is the True Remedy. If in this argument I have not unworthily vindicated Truth, then have I spoken according to my desires; if imperfectly, then only according to my powers. But there are other things, not belonging to the argument, which still press for utterance.

Sir, the people of Kansas, bone of your bone and flesh of your flesh, with the education of freemen and the rights of American citizens, now stand at your door. Will you send them away, or bid them enter ? Will you push them back to renew their struggles with a deadly foe, or will you preserve them in security and peace ? Will you cast them again into the den of Tyranny, or will you help their despairing efforts to escape ? These questions I put with no common solicitude; for I feel that on their just determination depend all the most precious interests of the Republic ; and I perceive too clearly the prejudices in the way, and the accumulating bitterness against this distant people, now claiming their simple birthright, while I am bowed with mortification, as I recognise the President of the United States, who should have been a staff to the weak, and a shield to the innocent, at the head of this strange oppression.

At every stage, the similitude between the wrongs of Kansas, and those other wrongs against which our fathers rose, becomes more apparent. Read the Declaration of Independence, and there is hardly an accusation which is there directed against the British Monarch, which may not now be directed with increased force against the American President. The parallel has a fearful particularity. Our fathers complained that the King had " sent hither swarms of officers, to harass our people, and eat out their substance ;" that he "had combined, with others, to subject us to a jurisdiction foreign to our Constitution, *giving his assent to their acts of pretended legislation ;*" that " he had abdicated government here, by declaring us out of his protection, and *waging war against us ;*" that " he had excited domestic insurrection among us, and *endeavoured to bring on the inhabitants of our frontier the merciless savages;* that our repeated petitions have been answered only by repeated injury." And this arraignment was aptly followed by the damning words, that " a Prince, whose character is thus marked by every act which may define a tyrant, is unfit to be the ruler of a free people." And surely, a President who has done all these things cannot be less unfit than a Prince. At every stage, the responsibility is brought directly to him. His offence has been both of commission and omission. He has done that which he ought not to have done, and he has left undone that which he ought to have done. By his activity the Prohibition of Slavery was overturned. By his failure to act, the honest emigrants in Kansas have been left a prey to wrong of all kinds. *Nullum flagitium extitit, nisi per te ; nullum flagitium sine te.* And now he stands forth the most conspicuous enemy of that unhappy Territory.

As the tyranny of the British King is all renewed

in the President, so on this floor have the old indig-
nities been renewed, which embittered and fomented
the troubles of our fathers. The early petition of
the American Congress to Parliament, long before
any suggestion of Independence, was opposed — like
the petitions of Kansas — because that body "was
assembled without any requisition on the part of
the Supreme Power." Another petition from New
York, presented by Edmund Burke, was flatly rejected, as claiming rights derogatory to Parliament.
And still another petition from Massachusetts Bay
was dismissed as "vexatious and scandalous," while
the patriot philosopher who bore it was exposed to
peculiar contumely. Throughout the debates, our
fathers were made the butt of sorry jests and super-
cilious assumptions. And now these scenes, with
these precise objections, have been renewed in the
American Senate.

With regret, I come again upon the Senator from
South Carolina [Mr. BUTLER], who, omnipresent in
this debate, overflowed with rage at the simple suggestion that Kansas had applied for admission as a
State; and, with incoherent phrases, discharged the
loose expectoration of his speech, now upon her representative, and then upon her people. There was
no extravagance of the ancient Parliamentary debate
which he did not repeat; nor was there any possible
deviation from truth which he did not make, with so
much of passion, I am glad to add, as to save him
from the suspicion of intentional aberration. But
the Senator touches nothing which he does not dis-
figure—with error, sometimes of principle, sometimes
of fact. He shows an incapacity of accuracy, whether in stating the Constitution or in stating the law,
whether in the details of statistics or the diversions
of scholarship. He cannot ope his mouth, but out

there flies a blunder. Surely he ought to be familiar with the life of Franklin ; and yet he referred to this household character, while acting as agent of our fathers in England, as above suspicion ; and this was done that he might give point to a false contrast with the agent of Kansas — not knowing that, however they may differ in genius and fame, in this experience they are alike : that Franklin, when intrusted with the petition of Massachusetts Bay, was assaulted by a foul-mouthed speaker, where he could not be heard in defence, and denounced as a "thief," even as the agent of Kansas has been assaulted on this floor, and denounced as a "forger." And let not the vanity of the Senator be inspired by the parallel with the British statesmen of that day ; for it is only in hostility to Freedom that any parallel can be recognised.

But it is against the people of Kansas that the sensibilities of the Senator are particularly aroused. Coming, as he announces, "from a State"— aye, sir, from South Carolina — he turns with lordly disgust from this newly-formed community, which he will not recognise even as "a body politic." Pray, sir, by what title does he indulge in this egotism ? Has he read the history of "the State" which he represents ? He cannot surely have forgotten its shameful imbecility from Slavery, confessed throughout the Revolution, followed by its more shameful assumptions for Slavery since. He cannot have forgotten its wretched persistance in the slave trade as the very apple of its eye, and the condition of its participation in the Union. He cannot have forgotten its Constitution, which is republican only in name, confirming power in the hands of the few, and founding the qualifications of its legislators on "a settled freehold estate or ten negroes." And yet the Senator, to whom that "State" has in part committed the guardianship of its good name, instead of moving, with backward treading steps, to cover its nakedness, rushes forward, in the very ecstasy of madness, to expose it, by provoking a comparison with Kansas. South Carolina is old; Kansas is young. South Carolina counts by centuries, where Kansas counts by years. But a beneficent example may be born in a day; and I venture to say, that against the two centuries of the older "State," may be already set two years of trial, evolving corresponding virtue, in the younger community. In the one is the long wail of Slavery; in the other, the hymns of Freedom. And if we glance at special achievements, it will be difficult to find anything in the history of South Carolina which presents so much of heroic spirit in an heroic cause as appears in that repulse of the Missouri invaders by the beleaguered town of Lawrence, where even the women gave their effective efforts to Freedom. The matrons of Rome, who poured their jewels into the treasury for the public defence — the wives of Prussia, who, with delicate fingers, clothed their defenders against French invasion; the mothers of our own Revolution, who sent forth their sons, covered over with prayers and blessings, to combat for Human Rights, did nothing of self-sacrifice truer than did these women on this occasion. Were the whole history of South Carolina blotted out of existence, from its very beginning down to the day of the last election of the Senator to his present seat on this floor, civilisation might lose — I do not say how little; but surely less than it has already gained by the example of Kansas, in its valiant struggle against oppression, and in the development of a new science of emigration. Already in Lawrence alone there are newspapers and schools, including a High School, and throughout this infant Territory there is more of mature scholarship, in proportion to its inhabitants, than in all South Carolina. Ah, sir, I tell the Senator that Kansas, welcomed as a Free State, will be a "ministering angel" to the Republic, when South Carolina, in the cloak of darkness which she hugs, "lies howling."

The Senator from Illinois [Mr. DOUGLAS] naturally joins the Senator from South Carolina in this warfare, and gives to it the superior intensity of his nature. He thinks that the National Government has not completely proved its power, as it has never hanged a traitor; but, if the occasion requires, he hopes there will be no hesitation; and this threat is directed at Kansas, and even at the friends of Kansas throughout the country. Again occurs the parallel with the struggles of our fathers, and I borrow the language of Patrick Henry, when, to the cry from the Senator, of "Treason," "Treason," I reply, "If this be treason, make the most of it." Sir, it is easy to call names; but I beg to tell the Senator that if the word "traitor" is in any way applicable to those who refuse submission to a tyrannical Usurpation, whether in Kansas or elsewhere, then must some new word, of deeper colour, be invented to designate those mad spirits who would endanger and degrade the Republic, while they betray all the cherished sentiments of the Fathers and the spirit of the Constitution, in order to give new spread to Slavery. Let the Senator proceed. It will not be the first time in history that a scaffold erected for punishment has become a pedestal of honour. Out of death comes life, and the "traitor" whom he blindly executes will live immortal in the cause.

"For Humanity sweeps onward; where to-day the martyr
   stands,
On the morrow crouches Judas, with the silver in his hands;
While the hooting mob of yesterday in silent awe return,
To glean up the scattered ashes into History's golden urn."

Among these hostile Senators, there is yet another,
with all the prejudices of the Senator from South
Carolina, but without his generous impulses, who, on
account of his character before the country, and the
rancour of his opposition, deserves to be named. I
mean the Senator from Virginia [Mr. MASON], who,
as the author of the Fugitive Slave Bill, has associated himself with a special act of inhumanity and
tyranny. Of him I shall say little, for he has said
little in this debate, though within that little was
compressed the bitterness of a life absorbed in the
support of Slavery. He holds the commission of Virginia; but he does not represent that early Virginia,
so dear to our hearts, which gave to us the pen of
Jefferson, by which the equality of men was declared,
and the sword of Washington, by which Independence
was secured; but he represents that other Virginia,
from which Washington and Jefferson now avert
their faces, where human beings are bred as cattle
for the shambles, and where a dungeon rewards the
pious matron who teaches little children to relieve
their bondage by reading the Book of Life. It is
proper that such a Senator, representing such a State,
should rail against Free Kansas.

But this is not all. The precedent is still more
clinching. Thus far I have followed exclusively the
public documents laid before Congress, and illustrated
by the debates of that body; but well-authenticated
facts, not of record here, make the case stronger still.
It is sometimes said that the proceedings in Kansas
are defective, because they originated in a party.

This is not true; but even if it were true, then would they still find support in the example of Michigan, where all the proceedings, stretching through successive years, began and ended in party. The proposed State Government was pressed by the Democrats as a *party test;* and all who did not embark in it were denounced. Of the Legislative Council, which called the first Constitutional Convention in 1835, all were Democrats; and in the Convention itself, composed of eighty-seven members, only seven were Whigs. The Convention of 1836, which gave the final assent, originated in a Democratic Convention on the 29th October, in the county of Wayne, composed of one hundred and twenty-four delegates, all Democrats, who proceeded to resolve —

" That the delegates of the *Democratic party* of Wayne, solemnly impressed with the spreading evils and dangers which a refusal to go into the Union has brought upon the people of Michigan, earnestly recommend meetings to be immediately convened by their fellow-citizens in every county of the State, with a view to the expression of their sentiments in favour of the election and call of another Convention, in time to secure our admission into the Union before the first of January next."

Shortly afterwards, a committee of five, appointed by this Convention, all leading Democrats, issued a circular, " under the authority of the delegates of the county of Wayne," recommending that the voters throughout Michigan should meet and elect delegates to a Convention to give the necessary assent to the Act of Congress. In pursuance of this call, the Convention met, and, as it originated in an exclusively party recommendation, so it was of an exclusively party character. And it was the action of this Convention that was submitted to Congress, and, after discussion in both bodies, on solemn votes, approved.

But the precedent of Michigan has another feature, which is entitled to the gravest attention, especially at this moment, when citizens engaged in the effort to establish a State Government in Kansas are openly arrested on the charge of treason, and we are startled by tidings of the maddest efforts to press this procedure of preposterous Tyranny. No such madness prevailed under Andrew Jackson; although, during the long pendency of the Michigan proceedings, for more than fourteen months, the Territorial Government was entirely ousted, and the State Government organised in all its departments. One hundred and thirty different legislative acts were passed, providing for elections, imposing taxes, erecting corporations, and establishing courts of justice, including a Supreme Court and a Court of Chancery. All process was issued in the name of the people of the State of Michigan. And yet no attempt was made to question the legal validity of these proceedings, whether legislative or judicial. Least of all did any menial Governor, dressed in a little brief authority, play the fantastic tricks which we now witness in Kansas; nor did any person wearing the robes of justice shock High Heaven with the mockery of injustice now enacted by the emissaries of the President in that Territory. No, sir; nothing of this kind then occurred. Andrew Jackson was President.

Senators such as these are the natural enemies of Kansas, and I introduce them with reluctance, simply that the country may understand the character of the hostility which must be overcome. Arrayed with them, of course, are all who unite, under any pretext or apology, in the propagandism of Human Slavery. To such, indeed, the time-honoured safeguards of popular rights can be a name only, and nothing more. What are trial by jury, habeas corpus, the ballot-box, the right of petition, the liberty of Kansas,—your liberty, sir, or mine,—to one who lends himself, not merely to the support at home, but to the propagandism abroad, of that preposterous wrong which denies even the right of a man to himself! Such a cause can be maintained only by a practical subversion of all rights. It is, therefore, merely according to reason that its partisans should uphold the Usurpation in Kansas.

To overthrow this Usurpation is now the special, importunate duty of Congress, admitting of no hesitation or postponement. To this end it must lift itself from the cabals of candidates, the machinations of party, and the low level of vulgar strife. It must turn from that Slave Oligarchy which now controls the Republic, and refuse to be its tool. Let its power be stretched forth towards this distant Territory, not to bind, but to unbind; not for the oppression of the weak, but for the subversion of the tyrannical; not for the prop and maintenance of a revolting Usurpation, but for the confirmation of Liberty.

"These are imperial arts, and worthy thee!"

Let it now take its stand between the living and dead, and cause this plague to be stayed. All this it *can* do: and if the interests of Slavery did not oppose, all this it *would* do at once, in reverent regard for justice, law, and order, driving far away all the alarms of war; nor would it dare to brave the shame and punishment of this Great Refusal. But the Slave Power dares anything; and it can be conquered only by the united masses of the People. From Congress to the People, I appeal.

Already Public Opinion gathers unwonted forces

to scourge the aggressors. In the press, in daily
conversation, wherever two or three are gathered
together, there the indignant utterance finds vent.
And trade, by unerring indications, attests the growing energy. Public credit in Missouri droops. The
six per cents of that State, which at par should be
102, have sunk to $84\frac{1}{4}$ — thus at once completing the
evidence of Crime, and attesting its punishment.
Business is now turning from the Assassins and
Thugs that infest the Missouri River on the way to
Kansas, to seek some safer avenue. And this, though
not unimportant in itself, is typical of greater changes.
The political credit of the men who uphold the
Usurpation, droops even more than the stocks; and
the People are turning from all those through whom
the Assassins and Thugs have derived their disgraceful
immunity.

It was said of old, " Cursed be he that removeth
his neighbour's Landmark. *And all the people shall
say, Amen.*"—(*Deut.* xxvii. 17.) Cursed, it is said,
in the city, and in the field; cursed in basket and
store ; cursed when thou comest in, and cursed when
thou goest out. These are terrible imprecations ; but
if ever any Landmark were sacred, it was that by
which an immense territory was guarded *for ever*
against Slavery ; and if ever such imprecations could
justly descend upon any one, they must descend now
upon all who, not content with the removal of this
sacred Landmark, have since, with criminal complicity, fostered the incursions of the great Wrong
against which it was intended to guard. But I utter
no imprecations. These are not my words ; nor is
it my part to add to or subtract from them. But,
thanks be to God ! they find a response in the hearts
of an aroused People, making them turn from every
man, whether President, or Senator, or Representative,

who has been engaged in this Crime—especially from those who, cradled in free institutions, are without the apology of education or social prejudice—until of all such those other words of the prophet shall be fulfilled — " I will set my face against that man, and make him a sign and a proverb, and I will cut him off from the midst of my people."— (*Ezekiel* xiv. 8.) Turning thus from the authors of this Crime, the People will unite once more with the Fathers of the Republic, in a just condemnation of Slavery—determined especially that it shall find no home in the National Territories — while the Slave Power, in which the Crime had its beginning, and by which it is now sustained, will be swept into the charnel-house of defunct Tyrannies.

In this contest, Kansas bravely stands forth — the stripling leader, clad in the panoply of American institutions. In calmly meeting and adopting a frame of Government, her people have with intuitive promptitude performed the duties of freemen ; and when I consider the difficulties by which she was beset, I find dignity in her attitude. *In offering herself for admission into the Union as a* FREE STATE, *she presents a single issue for the people to decide.* And since the Slave Power now stakes on this issue all its ill-gotten supremacy, the People, while vindicating Kansas, will at the same time overthrow this Tyranny. Thus does the contest which she now begins involve not only Liberty for herself, but for the whole country. God be praised, that she did not bend ignobly beneath the yoke ! Far away on the prairies, she is now battling for the Liberty of all, against the President, who misrepresents all. Everywhere among those who are not insensible to Right, the generous struggle meets a generous response. From innumerable throbbing hearts go forth the very words of encouragement which in the sorrowful days of our fathers, were sent by Virginia, speaking by the pen of Richard Henry Lee, to Massachusetts, in the person of her popular tribune, Samuel Adams :

"CHANTILLY, VA., *June* 23. 1774.

"I hope the good people of Boston will not lose their spirits, under their present heavy oppression, for they will certainly be supported by the other Colonies ; and the cause for which they suffer is so glorious and so deeply interesting to the present and future generations, that all America will owe, in a great measure, their political salvation to the present virtue of Massachusetts Bay."—(*American Archives, 4th series,* vol. i. p. 446.)

In all this sympathy there is strength. But in the cause itself there is angelic power. Unseen of men, the great spirits of History combat by the side of the people of Kansas, breathing a divine courage. Above all towers the majestic form of Washington once more, as on the bloody field, bidding them to remember those rights of Human Nature for which the War of Independence was waged. Such a cause, thus sustained, is invincible.

The contest which, beginning in Kansas, has reached us, will soon be transferred from Congress to a broader stage, where every citizen will be not only spectator, but actor ; and to their judgment I confidently appeal. To the people, now on the eve of exercising the electoral franchise, in choosing a Chief Magistrate of the Republic, I appeal, to vindicate the electoral franchise in Kansas. Let the ballot-box of the Union, with multitudinous might, protect the ballot-box in that Territory. Let the voters everywhere, while rejoicing in their own rights, help to guard the equal rights of distant fellow-citizens ; that the shrines of popular institutions, now desecrated, may be sanctified anew ; that the ballot-box, now plundered, may be restored ; and that the cry, " I am an American citizen," may not be sent forth in vain against outrage of every kind. In just regard for free labour in that Territory, which it is sought to blast by unwelcome association with slave labour ; in Christian sympathy with the slave, whom it is proposed to task and to sell there ; in stern condemnation of the Crime which has been consummated on that beautiful soil; in rescue of fellow-citizens, now subjugated to a tyrannical Usurpation; in dutiful respect for the Early Fathers, whose aspirations are now ignobly thwarted ; in the name of the Constitution, which has been outraged — of the Laws trampled down — of Justice banished — of Humanity degraded — of Peace destroyed — of Freedom crushed to earth ; and, in the name of the Heavenly Father, whose service is perfect Freedom, I make this last appeal.

The Answers to this speech contain some specimens of Transatlantic feeling.

" Is it," said Mr. Douglas, (*a candidate for the Presidency*) " the object of the Senator to provoke some of us to kick him as we would a dog in the street, that he may get sympathy upon the just chastisement ?

" The Senator, by his charge of crime, stultifies three-fourths of the whole body, a majority of the North, nearly the whole South, a majority of Whigs, and a majority of Democrats here. He says they are infamous. If he so believed, who could suppose that he would ever show his face among such a body of men ? How dare he approach one of those gentlemen to give him his hand after that act ? If he felt the courtesies between men he would not do it. He would deserve to have himself spit in the face for doing so.

" The attack of the Senator from Massachusetts now is not on me alone. Even the courteous and the accomplished Senator from South Carolina [Mr. Butler] could not be passed in his absence."

Mr. Mason—" Advantage was taken of it."

Mr. Douglas—" It is suggested that advantage is taken of his absence. I think that is a mistake. I think the speech was written and practised, and the gestures fixed; and if that part had been stricken out, the Senator would not have known how to repeat the speech. All that tirade of abuse must be brought down on the head of the venerable, the courteous, and the distinguished Senator from South Carolina. I shall not defend that gentleman

here.   He will be here in due time to speak for himself, and to act for himself, too.   I know what will
happen.   The Senator from Massachusetts will go to
him, whisper a secret apology in his ear, and ask
him to accept that as satisfaction for a public outrage
on his character!   I know how the Senator from
Massachusetts is in the habit of doing those things.
I have some experience of his skill in that respect."

Mr. MASON, of Virginia, said:

" Mr. President, the necessities of our political position bring us into relations and associations upon
this floor, which, in obedience to a common Government, we are forced to admit.   They bring us into
relations and associations which, beyond the walls of
this Chamber, we are enabled to avoid—associations
here, whose presence elsewhere is dishonour, and the
touch of whose hand would be a disgrace.

" The necessity of political position alone brings
me into relations with men upon this floor whom
elsewhere I cannot acknowledge as possessing man-
hood in any form.   I am constrained to hear here
depravity, vice in its most odious form uncoiled in
this presence, exhibiting its loathsome deformities in
accusation and vilification against the quarter of the
country from which I come; and I must listen to it
because it is a necessity of my position, under a common Government, to recognise as an equal, politically,
one whom to see elsewhere is to shun and despise.   I
did not intend to be betrayed into this debate; but
I submit to the necessity of my position.   I am here
now, united with an honoured band of patriots, from
the North equally with the South, to try if we can
preserve and perpetuate those institutions which
others are prepared to betray, and are seeking to
destroy; and I will submit to the necessity of that
position at least until the work is accomplished."

The outrage which followed is thus described in the Boston papers : —

FROM THE "BOSTON DAILY ADVERTISER," MAY 24.

"Our own correspondent at Washington was one of the few persons who were present in the Senate Chamber, eye-witnesses of the assault upon Mr. Sumner. His telegraphic despatch to us was, we believe, the first received in Boston, announcing the occurrence. We give below a letter from him received by mail last evening, written immediately after the affair.

" ' Washington, May 22. 1856.

" ' The Senate adjourned early to-day, in consequence of the announcement of the death of Hon. Mr. Miller, of Missouri. After the adjournment, as is the custom of many Senators, Mr. Sumner remained at his desk writing. There were also present Mr. Crittenden, of Kentucky, and several other Senators, who had not left the Chamber, some of the subordinate officers of the Senate, and a number of other persons, including your correspondent.

" ' While Mr. Sumner was thus seated writing, Mr. Preston S. Brooks, of South Carolina, entered the Chamber, accompanied by Mr. Keitt, of the same State—both members of the House of Representatives. These approached Mr. Sumner's seat, when the former raised a cane some three-quarters of an inch or an inch in diameter, and struck Mr. Sumner a severe blow over the head with it. Mr. Sumner sprang from his seat, but staggered under the effect of the blow, reeling about and falling partially over the desk. Notwithstanding his helpless condition, the chivalric

South Carolinian repeated his blows with great force and rapidity.

"'Senator Crittenden, of Kentucky—than whom the South has no braver or more chivalric son — did not hesitate to pronounce the assault a *shameful outrage* —a remark which suggested a significant glance from Keitt to Brooks—to which the latter replied by saying, "Well, *one will do !*" I know not what else was the meaning of this expression, except that the parties were tempted to try their prowess upon the aged Crittenden, but concluded not to venture it.

"'Mr. Sumner, who lay upon the floor in a state of partial stupor, in consequence of the blows inflicted upon his head, was raised by his friends, and carried into the anteroom of the Chamber, where medical service was promptly procured. Although his head is badly contused and severely cut, it is hoped that the wounds are not dangerous, although at the same time it is difficult to judge with certainty. The entire assault, of course, occupied but a minute or two. Your correspondent was standing just inside the corner door of the Chamber — some twenty feet from the parties—when the assault was commenced, but by the time himself and the friend with whom he was conversing could reach the spot, the thing was over. The mad rage of the assailant may be judged from the fact that he broke his cane into fragments.'"

FROM THE "NEW YORK EVENING POST," MAY 23.

"Washington, May 22.

"There were at least a dozen persons standing near at the time of the assault, which was so unexpected that, as they say, they did not think of interfering. Close by stood, as I am informed, the Senate's Sergeant-at-Arms, a large, strong man, and yet he did nothing. Mr. Crittenden came forward from another part of the Hall, and denounced the attack, to the perpetrator, with the manly indignation characteristic of the chivalrous veteran of Kentucky, as a 'shameless transaction.'   But the reply was, I am told, 'You'd better not interfere, we will lick one at a time.' Keitt stood by with a cane, ready to save Brooks from injury ; many persons having the impression that he was armed, though no fire-arms were displayed, either by him or Brooks.

"Mr. Sumner's legs, at the time when he was attacked, were under the desk, so far that he could only rise by wrenching it from the floor.   The stunning, sudden force of the blow knocked his head forward.   His assailant then, seizing him by the shoulder, held him with his left hand while with the other he kept laying the blows upon his head."

" MR. SUMNER'S STATEMENT.

"The following is the statement of Mr. Sumner, under oath:

" I attended the Senate as usual on Thursday, the 22nd of May. After some formal business, a message was received from the House of Representatives, announcing the death of a member of that body from Missouri. This was followed by a brief tribute to the deceased from Mr. Geyer, of Missouri, when, according to usage and out of respect to the deceased, the Senate adjourned at once. Instead of leaving the Senate Chamber with the rest of the Senators, on the adjournment, I continued in my seat, occupied with my pen, and while thus intent, in order to be in season for the mail, which was soon to close, I was approached by several persons who desired to converse with me, but I answered them promptly and briefly, excusing myself for the reason that I was much engaged. When the last of these persons left me I drew my arm-chair close to my desk, and with my legs under the desk continued writing. My attention at this time was so entirely drawn from all other subjects that, though there must have been many persons in the Senate, I saw nobody. While thus intent, with my head bent over my writing, I was addressed by a person who approached the front of my desk; I was so entirely absorbed that I was not aware of his presence until I heard my name pronounced. As I looked up with pen in hand, I saw a tall man, whose countenance was not familiar, standing directly over me, and at the same moment caught these words : ' I have read your speech twice over carefully; it is a libel on South Carolina, and Mr. Butler, who is a relative of mine.' While these words were still passing from his lips, he commenced a succession of blows with a heavy cane on my bare head, by the first of which I was stunned so as to lose my sight. I saw no longer my assailant, nor any other person or object in the room. What I did afterward was done almost unconsciously, acting under the instincts of self-defence. With head already bent down, I rose from my seat — wrenching up my desk, which was screwed to the floor—and then pressing forward, while my assailant continued his blows. I had no other consciousness until I found myself ten feet forward in front of my desk, lying on the floor of the Senate, with my bleeding head supported on the knee of a gentleman whom I soon recognised by voice and manner as Mr. Morgan, of New York. Other persons there were about me offering me friendly assistance, but I did not recognise any of them. Others there were at a distance, looking on and offering no assistance, of whom I recognised only Mr. Douglas, of Illinois, Mr. Toombs, of Georgia, and I thought also my assailant standing between them. I was helped from the floor and conducted into the lobby of the Senate, where I was placed upon a sofa. Of those who helped me here I have no recollection. As I entered the lobby I recognised Mr. Slidell, of Louisiana, who retreated, but I recognised no one else until I felt a friendly grasp of the hand, which seemed to come from Mr. Campbell, of Ohio. I have a vague impression that Mr. Bright, President of the Senate, spoke to me while I was on the floor of the Senate or in the lobby. I make this statement in answer to the interrogatory of the Committee, and offer it as presenting completely all my recollections of the assault and of the attending circumstances, whether immediately before or immediately after. I desire to add, that beside the words which I have given as uttered by my assailant, I have an indistinct recollection of the words ' old man '; but these are so enveloped in the mist which ensued from the first blow, that I am not sure whether they were uttered or not.

" On the cross-examination of Mr. Sumner he stated that he was entirely without arms of any kind, and that he had no notice or warning of any kind, direct or indirect, of this assault."

The last set of documents which appear to deserve publication are the comments of the American writers and speakers.

FROM THE " RICHMOND INQUIRER," JUNE 12.

" In the main, the press of the South applaud the conduct of Mr. Brooks, without condition or limitation. Our approbation, at least, is entire and unreserved. We consider the act good in conception, better in execution, and best of all in consequence. The vulgar Abolitionists in the Senate are getting above themselves. They have been humoured until they forget their position. They have grown saucy, and dare to be impudent to gentlemen ! Now, they are a low, mean, scurvy set, with some little book learning, but as utterly devoid of spirit or honour as a pack of curs. Intrenched behind ' privilege,' they fancy they can slander the South, and insult its representatives with impunity. The truth is, they

have been suffered to run too long without collars.
They must be lashed into submission. Sumner, in
particular, ought to have nine-and-thirty early every
morning. He is a great strapping fellow, and could
stand the cowhide beautifully. Brooks frightened
him, and at the first blow of the cane he bellowed
like a bull-calf. There is the blackguard Wilson, an
ignorant Natick cobbler, swaggering in excess of
muscle, and absolutely dying for a beating. Will
not somebody take him in hand? Hale is another
huge, red-faced, sweating scoundrel, whom some
gentleman should kick and cuff until he abates something of his impudent talk. These men are perpetu-
ally abusing the people and representatives of the
South, for tyrants, robbers, ruffians, adulterers, and
what not. Shall we stand it? Can gentlemen sit
still in the Senate and House of Representatives,
under an incessant stream of denunciation from
wretches who avail themselves of the privilege of
place to indulge their devilish passions with impunity? In the absence of an adequate law, Southern
gentlemen must protect their own honour and feelings. It is an idle mockery to challenge one of these
scullions. It is equally useless to attempt to disgrace
them. They are insensible to shame, and can be
brought to reason only by an application of cowhide
or gutta percha. Let them once understand that for
every vile word spoken against the South, they will
suffer so many stripes, and they will soon learn to
behave themselves like decent dogs — they can never
be gentlemen. Mr. Brooks has initiated this salutary
discipline, and he deserves applause for the bold,
judicious manner in which he chastised the scamp
Sumner. It was a proper act, done at the proper
time, and in the proper place.

  "Of all places on earth, the Senate Chamber, the

theatre of his vituperative exploits, was the very spot where Sumner should have been made to suffer for his violation of the decencies of decorous debate, and for his brutal denunciation of a venerable statesman. It was literally and entirely proper that he should be stricken down and beaten just beside the desk against which he leaned as he fulminated his filthy utterances through the Capitol. It is idle to talk of the sanctity of the Senate Chamber, since it is polluted by the presence of such fellows as Wilson, and Sumner, and Wade. They have desecrated it, and cannot now fly to it as to a sanctuary from the lash of vengeance.

" We trust other gentlemen will follow the example of Mr. Brooks, that so a curb may be imposed upon the truculence and audacity of Abolition speakers. If need be, let us have a caning or cowhiding every day. If the worst come to the worst, so much the sooner, so much the better."

A MEETING IN SOUTH CAROLINA.

" A public meeting of the citizens of Fairfield was held on Tuesday night, 27th ult., to approve the conduct of the Hon. Preston S. Brooks, in administering to Charles Sumner, of Massachusetts, a wholesome and richly merited castigation.

" On motion of Mr. G. H. McMaster, James M. Rutland, Esq., was called to the chair, and S. R. Stirling appointed Secretary.

" The object of the meeting being briefly stated by Franklin Gaillard, James R. Aiken, Esq., offered the following preamble and resolutions, which he handsomely sustained by remarks adapted to the occasion:

"'Whereas the citizens of the slaveholding States have for many years practically submitted to the most aggravated ex-

pressions of insolence and abuse from citizens of the Northern
States, as disseminated not only from the press, but also from
the pulpit and the forum; and whereas a tame and quiet submission to such limited conceptions of truth, justice, and
equity only tend to degrade the South from her high position
and deprive her of those constitutional rights which she has
ever maintained at any and every sacrifice—

"'Resolved, That we most heartily approve the practical
enforcement of respect for the motives of Southern men and
Southern States, in the chastisement inflicted upon the cham-
pion of black republicanism by the Hon. P. S. Brooks; and
that we hereby tender to Mr. Brooks our cordial approbation
of his gallantry, and express our indignation at the spirit manifested, not only by Abolition orators and papers, but by the
public meetings in Northern cities, which have undertaken
to denounce his course on the above occasion.

"That a special delegate be sent to Washington to carry
a copy of these proceedings.

"That the Secretary be requested to forward by him a
copy to each of our delegates in Congress.'

"The meeting was addressed by Gen. John Bucha-
nan and Major James H. Rion."

FROM THE "SOUTH SIDE DEMOCRAT," MAY 24.

"The telegraph has recently announced no information more grateful to our feelings than the *classical*
caning which this outrageous Abolitionist received,
on Thursday, at the hands of the chivalrous Brooks,
of South Carolina. It is enough for *gentlemen* to bear
to be compelled to associate with such a character as
Sumner, and to be bored with the stupid and arrogant dogmas with which his harangues invariably
abound; but when, in gross violation of Senatorial
courtesy and in defiance of public opinion, the unscrupulous Abolitionist undertakes to heap upon the
head of a venerable Senator a vulgar tirade of abuse

and calumny, no punishment is adequate to a proper restraint of his insolence but a deliberate, cool, dignified, and *classical* caning."

FROM THE "BALTIMORE REPUBLICAN," MAY 24.

"*The Flogging of a Demagogue.*—Not a few tender-footed people of our city have professed fears of great excitement at the North, growing out of the deserved chastisement of a foul-mouthed demagogue. These forget that the disposition to resent bestial insult and wrong is not less prevalent at the North than in our own latitude. The spirited men of the North, who have long sickened into loathing with inflictions of Abolition vituperation, will fail to see, in the circumstances attending the flogging of a pre-eminent blackguard, much to distinguish it from the usual cases of personal retribution. Indeed, they have ever been amazed at the degree of personal consideration which has been extended to red-handed foes of the South by those whose personal characters are so ruthlessly assailed. To this they justly attribute much of the consequence which fanaticism has reached in the Free States. The remedy is obvious, and should be promptly administered. Beyond respectful official recognition, non-intercourse with Abolitionists — the practice of Mr. Calhoun — should be adopted. No greater service to the Northern supporters of the Constitution and the Union could possibly be done. It was to be expected that an attempt would be essayed by the Abolitionists to make political capital out of the transaction. Doubtless the flagellation was tamely received for the same reason. But there is nothing in the public tone that looks to serious consequences, while a large portion of the press of the North set the provocation fully before the people."

"The 'South Carolina Times' (State Paper), of the 27th ult., holds the following language in relation to the late attack on Mr. Sumner:—

"Up to the 22nd of May, A. D. 1856, none have been found willing to step forward, as Carolinians, in defence of the character of Southern men or the institutions of the South, but the Hon. Preston S. Brooks. He, on that memorable day, rallying none to his support, confronted, in the Senate Chamber, the unprincipled Abolitionist and rowdy, Charles Sumner, of Massachusetts, and rewarded him for his dastardly libel upon Senator Butler, and slander of the people of the South. Col. Brooks has the honour of being the first man who dared to carry out his declaration that he was ready to commence the war in Washington, in the halls of Congress.

"Colonel Brooks has done nothing that South Carolinians ought to be ashamed of. He has boldly stepped forward, at the risk of his life, ease, and social relation, in defence of the chivalrous Butler, and we know that there will be found but one sentiment among the people of South Carolina, which is 'Well done, thou good and faithful servant.'"

The following resolution was passed at a late meeting of the citizens of Newberry (Brooks's district):

"Be it unanimously resolved, That this meeting approves the conduct of the Hon. P. S. Brooks in the premises, and that it recommends that meetings be held, on the first Monday in June next, in the various districts constituting this Congressional district, to express the approbation which we are sure his constituents generally will accord to him."

FROM THE " NEW YORK EVENING POST" OF THE
11TH JUNE 1856.

Extract from a speech by Mr. Richard Dana, ju-
nior *, at a Sumner meeting in Cambridge held in
June 1856 : —

" Charles Sumner has been struck down in a manner which his colleague has for ever branded, and so
we declare it to-night, as 'brutal, murderous, and
cowardly.' This is bad, but it is not that which stirs
the people of the free States as one man. He was
struck down for words spoken in debate, and in the
sanctuary of his office.

" But this is not all. It was done by a member of
Congress, and expressly for words spoken in debate.
But this is not half. It will not be punished. The
man who did the deed will not be expelled, nor will
he be punished, adequately, if at all, by the laws of
the District of Columbia, — a domain ceded to Congress for the very purpose of enabling it to secure
freedom of debate and action, by laws of its own. All
this may seem bad, wrong, grievous, intolerable. But
I have not begun to name the great evil yet. There
are ninety representatives from the Slave States.
Every one present at the vote, voted against inquiry.
There were several senators from the Slave States present at the assault. Blow after blow fell on his defenceless head. No one knew that the next blow might not
be the fatal blow ; yet no one interfered ; no word, no
cry, no motion. [Yes, Mr. Crittenden did.] Perhaps
he did, at the close, a little, but for that little he was
threatened with chastisement on the spot. Not one
press south of the Potomac has condemned the act.

* The Author of " Two Years before the Mast."

M

Not one public man, or public body, has condemned
it.   On the contrary, all have adopted and defended
it.   It is recognised as a policy — as a system — and
commendation and honour are heaped upon the perpetrator, so that others may be stimulated to do
the like.   Already the leading southern journals are
pointing out the next victim.   A kind of Lynch law
is to be instituted wherever the subject of slavery is
involved.

" Now, fellow-citizens, I beg you to ask yourselves
what all this indicates.   Let us not be children, gazing
at the painted scene; let us lift the curtain and look
at the movers and actors behind.

" Freedom of speech is at stake in Congress.   Freedom in the choice of institutions is at stake in Kansas.   Seven in every eight of the inhabitants of Kansas desire free institutions ; yet slavery is forced upon
them.   The people cannot select their institutions, nor
can Congress prescribe them.   Force governs — irre-
gular, unlawful, brute-force governs ; and governs by
aid and countenance of the national authorities !

" Mr. President, the last census has demonstrated
what many have declared, but few have believed, that
under the form of a republic, this country is now,
and has long been, governed by an oligarchy.   In the
free states there are now about seventeen millions of
free inhabitants and no slaves.   In the slave states
there are four millions of slaves, owned by three hundred and fifty thousand owners.   These 350,000
owners of slaves own the valuable land and the labourers, and monopolise the government of the Slave
States.   The non-slaveholding free population is of
little account.   This forms the privileged class, the
oligarchy.   It is not for the purpose of making them
odious that I use this name.   It is the only proper
designation.   Including the families of the owners,

there may be two millions of persons in the dominant class or order.

" This oligarchy has governed the whole country, and governs it now with a sway of increasing demands and exactions. Of seventeen presidential elections, natives of Slave States have carried thirteen, and natives of Free States four. Of the life of our government, forty-nine years have been passed under slaveholding chief-magistrates, and eighteen under non-slaveholders. They have always had a majority of the judges of the Supreme Court of the United States. The population, the arts, the sciences, commerce, inventions, copyrights, manufactures, all are with the Free States. Yet the Slave States hold and have always held the judiciary. They almost monopolised the army and navy when appointments were open. At this moment, though there are sixteen Free States and fifteen Slave States, a majority of the Senate are slave holders.

" To make a long story short, there has never been a question between the slave power and the free power, on the floor of Congress, in which the slave power has not triumphed.

" I will not go over the recital of the successive defeats of freedom and aggressions of slavery. The subjugation of Kansas is the latest triumph. The subjugation of free speech is its object now. At first, you recollect, no man can have forgotten, the right of petition was denied. For that John Quincy Adams perilled all a public man has to peril, and life itself. Next, through resolves of Congress and platforms of both the great parties, they tried again to suppress free speech. Now, they chastise it by violence, in the very sanctuary of its refuge. No man has received a national nomination that is not acceptable to them. No man can be confirmed in a national office, from

Secretary of State or Minister at St. James's to the humblest postmaster, that is not satisfactory to them. Mr. Everett's appointment at St. James's hung in suspense because he was suspected of having uttered, somewhere, a sentiment hostile to slavery and its interests. The country is one vast Dionysius's ear. Every whisper in the closet is transmitted and punished.

Before parting to-night, let me ask any doubting friend, if there be one here, what provocation more he proposes to wait for? They have added slave states by a *coûp d'état;* will you wait until they have added Cuba or Central America? They have tried to force slavery on Kansas; will you wait until they have succeeded? They have violated one solemn compact; how many more must they violate, before you will assert your right? They have struck down a senator in his place. Some of their presses have designated the next victim; will you wait until he has fallen?"

Mr. Dana was right. Mr. Brooks was not expelled from the Senate. His only punishment was a fine of 300 dollars. This is the value set in Washington on freedom of debate. Any ruffian willing to pay 60*l.* may waylay and disable an opponent.

THE END.

LONDON:
Printed by SPOTTISWOODE & Co.,
New-street-Square.